WHAT IS AN EVANGELICAL?

WHAT IS AN EVANGELICAL?

D. M. Lloyd-Jones

THE BANNER OF TRUTH TRUST

THE BANNER OF TRUTH TRUST
3 Murrayfield Road, Edinburgh EH12 6EL, UK
PO Box 621, Carlisle, PA 17013, USA

*

First published 1992
Reprinted 2002
Reprinted in new format 2016

*

ISBN
Print: 978 0 85151 626 4
EPUB: 978 1 84871 667 4
Kindle: 978 1 84871 668 1

*

Typeset in 11/15 pt Adobe Garamond Pro at
The Banner of Truth Trust, Edinburgh
Printed in the USA by
Versa Press, Inc.,
East Peoria, IL.

Contents

I

II

III

I

Jude, the servant of Jesus Christ, and brother of James, to them that are sanctified by God the Father, and preserved in Jesus Christ, and called: mercy unto you, and peace, and love, be multiplied. Beloved, when I gave all diligence to write unto you of the common salvation, it was needful for me to write unto you, and exhort you that ye should earnestly contend for the faith which was once delivered unto the saints (Jude 1-3).

T HIS, as most of you realize, is a very interesting statement, for it is rather unusual in the New Testament. Here Jude is telling the people to whom he is writing that his original intention was to write a letter giving an exposition of the common salvation of the Christian faith, something similar or analogous, one imagines, to what the apostle Paul did in the Epistle to the Romans. That was what he intended to do, but he tells them here that he was not able to do so, that his great purpose had to be laid on one side. Why was this? It was because news had come to him of certain attacks upon the faith so that, in a sense, what he is saying is this: We have not the time, nor can we afford to enjoy the luxury of just expounding the truth and taking our time over it as we do so. A very urgent matter has arisen and all of us must now contend earnestly for the faith. And that is what Jude does and that is the reason why it is such a short letter.

Now I take this as my general text for these three lectures or talks which I propose to give. Nothing would give me personally greater pleasure than to take a verse or passage of Scripture and expound it. Nothing gives me greater joy at any time than to do that, but I believe we are now in a position which is very similar to that in which this man Jude and others found themselves. A situation has arisen which compels us to consider the whole of the faith, and to defend the whole of the faith, urgently, and that is what I am going to try to do now with you.

I am proposing, in other words, to deal with the question, What is an evangelical? In the time of Jude this was the fundamental question which had arisen: What is the faith? What is a Christian? He says it is no use leisurely going over particular aspects of truth and of doctrine when the *whole* situation is being attacked and undermined. We have got to go back to the foundation, to the very basis. And I believe that we are now once more in such a situation. This is something that has arisen from time to time in the long history of the Christian church. Repeatedly, men and women in the church have had to go back to the origins, to define again and defend the very essence of the Christian faith.

The Constant Necessity for Definition

Now we are going to look at it in terms of 'What is an evangelical?' for we are meeting together under the auspices of the International Fellowship of *Evangelical* Students. There is the specific term. I want to try to show you that the situation today is such that we must not take this term 'evangelical' for granted. We must rediscover its meaning. We must define it again. And we must be ready to fight for it and to defend it.

There are those who might disagree with this and believe that there is no need to do this. They say, We all know what an evangelical is; it's a familiar term. In their view, as long as a man makes certain statements he is an evangelical, or if an organization makes certain positive statements, that organization is evangelical. I suggest that that is no longer true and that a situation has developed, and is continuing to develop, in which the whole question of the meaning of 'evangelical' has been thrown again into the melting pot. We must be sure and certain that we know exactly what we mean when we employ this term.

Why is this necessary? Well, my first answer would be that the history of the past, the history of the church throughout the centuries, shows very clearly that there is nothing static in the life of the church. There is always a process of change and of development, and unfortunately, as is true of nature, the process is generally one of degeneration. This, of course, is one of the main results of sin and of the fall. Sin has brought an element of degeneration into the life of man, and as a result of that, into the life of creation; so that even in the church herself there will be this tendency. In the New Testament you already see heresy, false teaching arising, subtle changes taking place with regard to what the Christian truth really is. The apostle Paul, in his great address to the elders of the church at Ephesus, as recorded in Acts 20, warns them of how, from among themselves, men will arise and teach false doctrines. Wolves, as it were, will come in and do harm to the flock of God. And this has continued ever since in the history of the church.

I shall never forget reading nearly forty years ago the opening sentence in a book on the subject of Protestantism. The first sentence reads thus: 'Every institution tends to produce its opposite.' That was the author's opening sentence in a book on Protestantism, and the thesis of the book, of course, was to point out – and he was able to do it very simply – that the position of most of the Protestant churches today is almost the exact opposite of their position when they originally came into being. I could easily take up the time in showing you this. Take Martin Luther and the beginnings of Protestantism as an example. You may remember how, in less than a hundred years from the rise of Lutheranism, there developed what we know as Lutheran scholasticism. A hardening process took place, subtle changes came in, so that by the middle of the seventeenth century Lutheranism presented a picture which was really very different from its origin under Luther. And the whole of the pietist movement with Spener and Arndt was a protest against this and an attempt to bring the church back to her origins.

The same thing happened among the reformed people: a hardening process took place; an intellectualism came in, so that you were soon confronted by something that had departed very seriously from the original position.

I could easily demonstrate this in the history of every denomination that is known to me personally, and of denominations and religious bodies in various other countries. This is a principle which we have got to recognize. It is no use assuming that because a thing has started correctly it is going to continue to be correct. There is a process at work, because of sin and evil, which tends to produce not only change but even degeneration.

Nor is this all. There is something further to point out as we look at the history of the church throughout the centuries. It is that this process of change is never a sudden one. It is always a subtle and slow process. You remember our Lord's own comparison about moth and rust. Rusting is a very slow process and if you do not watch out it will have developed in such an insidious manner that the first you know about it is that a girder on a bridge, or something like that, is broken. The change is almost imperceptible, and it is the same with the effect of a moth in a piece of clothing.

Perhaps the clearest demonstration of this that one can give is what happened in the last century, the nineteenth century, in connection with the so-called Higher Critical movement. At the beginning of that century there were a number of evangelical denominations and bodies. Then gradually a change came in, a change of emphasis, a change of teaching, but the striking thing about it was the slowness and the subtlety with which it came.

There were, of course, men who were very extreme, and who made bold statements, and almost everybody could see that they were wrong. They did not do the harm. They never do the harm. The obvious, open, arrogant heretic generally produces a reaction, and he is not the dangerous person.

The really dangerous man is the man who introduces some very slight or very subtle change. Now you will forgive me for giving an illustration out of the story of the church in the United Kingdom. It is, of course, the story with which I am most familiar, but the same thing could be demonstrated in the history of the church in America and other countries. There was a teacher in Scotland called A. B. Davidson. This is the kind of man who really did the harm. He was a professor in Old Testament and Hebrew, and he did the harm in this way. He was a very pious man, a very kindly man, and a very good man, with the result that most of his students did not realize that he was introducing a new element into his teaching as a result of accepting the Higher Criticism.

I remember a few years back noticing a thing which, if it had not been tragic, would have amused me very much. The centenary of the birth of this man, A. B. Davidson, was being celebrated, and I read two articles on him in the same week: one in a very liberal religious weekly, and the other in an evangelical religious weekly. They both praised him. The liberal paper praised him because he was the man who, above all others, had introduced the new 'scholarly view' of the Old Testament, and had accepted the Wellhausen scheme and all the rest of it; so they praised him. But an evangelical writer was also praising him, and praising him for his devotional spirit and that he always started his theological lectures by praying. Now this is the sort of man who has generally done the greatest harm because, to all appearances, and if you looked simply on the surface, you could not see any change at all. It was the little things which he kept on introducing which were the real danger.

Now the great Charles Haddon Spurgeon saw all this, but when he began to denounce what he called the 'Downgrade' movement he was attacked ferociously by evangelical people. They said, What is the matter with Mr Spurgeon? He's become hypercritical; he's turning molehills into mountains; he's exaggerating! History has proved that he was not exaggerating. He saw these subtle changes. Others said of the men whose influence Spurgeon feared, They are still evangelical; they say this and they say that, but they are truly evangelical. They did not pay attention to some of the other things that these men were beginning to say, and therefore they missed the very subtle process which was insinuating itself into the life of the churches.

Recent History and Changes

I want to suggest that we are confronted today by this self-same process and that even in the last ten years a very serious situation has arisen among evangelical people. My whole contention is that for us to assume that because we have once said that we are evangelical, therefore we must still be evangelical now ana shall always be, is not only to misread the teaching of the New Testament, but to fail completely to grasp and to understand the great lessons which are taught us so clearly by history.

Let me further substantiate what I am saying. You have in America something which boasts the name of the 'new evangelicalism'; it is even announcing itself to you. A 'new evangelicalism' – it is no longer the old. There is a sugges-tion of some difference, whatever it may be. The people who belong to this school produce books, and it is my contention that these books show this very subtle change in the defini-tion of what it means to be an evangelical. This change is not confined to America or to the term 'new evangelicalism'.

There are other particular instances I can give you. There was a great evangelical church in the United States called the Missouri Synod of the Lutheran Church. The Lutheran Church in the States is divided into a number of different bodies, but of all these divisions of Lutheranism, the *evan-gelical* body was the Missouri Synod. It was started in about 1860 by a German preacher and theologian by the name of Carl Walther. The Missouri Synod had stood throughout the years as a great bulwark of evangelicalism, but that is no longer true. Today, the Missouri Synod is in the midst of a serious conflict. It is divided more or less into two big groups. The subtle process, has taken place, and they are in the throes of a great debate in an attempt to determine what is really evangelical and what is not.

Take another example from the United States. There is the denomination known as the Christian Reformed Church, with its headquarters in Grand Rapids in Michigan. Here again is a great denomination that has stood throughout the years as a defender of evangelicalism. They have a college and a seminary, Calvin College and Calvin Theological Seminary. They have Christian schools. They were once a body of evangelical people who stood united in the defence of the historic faith. But that is no longer true. The Christian Reformed Church is now divided right down the centre, and a debate is going on there, again in an attempt to determine what is evangelical. Can you introduce certain changes and still say that you are the same, that you are still evangelical? That is the question which lies behind the conflict there at this present time.

Then perhaps a still more striking illustration of the same thing is what is happening in Holland in connection with the Free University. You are familiar, I am sure, with something of the history of the Free University started by Abraham Kuyper in 1880. It was in order to defend the evangelical faith that he founded this university. Most of us here this morning who are over a certain age, and who are connected with the IFES, have throughout the years looked to the Free University for the defence of our evangelical position. But you can no longer do that. A change has come in the Free University of Amsterdam just as it has come in these bodies in the United States which I have mentioned. The Free University and its denomination are no longer where they were even ten years ago. Then they were outside the ecumenical movement and the World Council; now they are inside. And not only that. In the books and articles of Free University teachers there are plain and obvious demonstrations of a very subtle change, a change not only of emphasis but of belief with regard to certain vital and essential matters.

I am emphasizing the subtlety of the change. As it has always been in the past, so it is today. Some people are saying, But you're exaggerating; these men are still making great Christian affirmations; what right have you to say that they are changing? My answer is that these changes always happen in this subtle way; but let me add to that.

This kind of change has another characteristic and this again has been proved from New Testament times right down to this day. At the beginning the changes generally take place on the periphery and not at the centre. This, again, is a part of the subtlety of the process. You do not find men suddenly making different statements about certain central truths; the difference begins with something right on the outside. And because the change generally begins there, some people argue that there has been no change at all. They say, These men are all right on the great central matters. But no, although change may begin somewhere outside, on the circumference, *that* is the serious aspect of the matter, for this reason, that Christian truth is *one*. It is the glory of the Christian truth that it has many parts, but they are all interrelated. What the apostle Paul says about the church in 1 Corinthians 12, where he compares it to a body, is equally true with regard to the body or the corpus of the Christian faith. Every part belongs to every other part, and the result is that if you make what appears to be a minor change somewhere on the circumference it will soon have its effect even upon the centre. And again, as I have said, this is a principle that one could easily illustrate in the long history of the Christian church.

Re-examining Our Name

Here then are considerations which make it imperative for us to re-examine our whole position. So many of the men who have undergone a great change in recent years, some of whom admit it openly, would still try to claim that they are truly evangelical. Therefore the problem is this: to define exactly what an evangelical is, and who exactly is evangelical.

I remember when we were beginning the IFES twenty-five, twenty-six years ago, that we were confronted by this same problem. We found that on the continent of Europe there was a tendency among some to regard anybody who was not a Roman Catholic as an evangelical. The use of the term evangelical was much broader, wider, and looser than it was in the case of Great Britain or America. There was a tendency to divide the religious situation into Roman Catholic and evangelical, and all who were not Catholic were automatically and inevitably evangelical. Now that is clearly much too broad a definition.

We must start by saying that the term evangelical is obviously a limiting term. I am not here this morning and on these subsequent mornings to discuss with you, What is a Christian? That is not what we are discussing. We are discussing, What is an evangelical? We, here in IFES, do not belong to a Christian body in that broad sense only. Of course we are Christian, but we claim to be evangelical Christians; that is what we are discussing together. There are individual Roman Catholics who are undoubtedly Christian. We are not discussing that.

Now if you use the term evangelical, obviously it has got some meaning. It is a limiting term. It is exclusive in certain respects. It puts certain things out, it emphasizes certain other things, and it is with this that I am concerned. I hope that this is quite clear. We are not simply defining the Christian in general, but we are defining the evangelical Christian, and we do that, of course, because we believe that ultimately the evangelical faith is the only true expression in doctrine of the Christian faith itself. You can be a Christian and yet defective in your doctrine, but our concern and our endeavour is to have the true doctrine presented in its fullness because we believe that it is only as this is believed and preached and propagated that men and women are going to be converted and added to the church. When the church has gone wrong in doctrine, she has ceased to be a converting influence. Here again is something that stands out very clearly in the long history of the church. That is why we should be so concerned about defining the meaning of this term evangelical and defending it even to our very 'latest breath'.

How, then, do we define the *evangelical* as distinct from the Christian in general ? Here is the great question today, and I think you will find it to be the question you will have to face increasingly in these coming years. You are probably already having to do so in the various countries to which you belong. Where does one set the limits? Now as we come to this it seems to me there are two main dangers confronting us, and .again I am saying this on the basis of the history of the past.

The Danger of Wrong Divisions

The first danger is to be too narrow, too rigid, and too detailed in definition. I call this a danger for the reason that it leads to what is called schism. What is schism? The best definition you will ever find of schism is in Paul's First Epistle to the Corinthians, especially in chapter 12 perhaps but it is also there in other places. Schism as it is defined by the great apostle is this: it is men and women who are agreed about

13

the centralities of the faith disagreeing about things which are not essential; it is a tearing of the body. The only man who can be guilty of schism, therefore, is a man who believes the truth, the essential truth, but denies other things which are not essential.

Let me give you examples from the church at Corinth to illustrate what I mean. The church at Corinth was divided up into groups and factions. The church was guilty of schism. What were they dividing over? Let me remind you of some of the things which the apostle indicates. They were dividing up over their favourite preachers: some said, 'I am of Paul'; others said, 'I am of Apollos'; others said, 'I am of Cephas'. Here were people who were agreed about the centralities of the Christian faith, who were not only dividing but quarrelling over their favourite preachers and forming their groups, separating from one another over such matters as the excellences of the various leaders.

Another cause of division was the question of possession of intellect and of understanding. There were some more enlightened people there, and they could see that there was nothing wrong in eating meats which had been offered to idols. To them there was nothing wrong in it because the idol is imaginary; it has no being. Though meat has been offered to an idol in a temple, that obviously does nothing at all to the meat, because there is nothing there to taint it. That was their position, and they were eating this meat and justifying themselves in doing so. But then there were weaker brethren who could not see this. They were tied by tradition, by their background, and this practice was an offence to them, and they were dividing over it. They were agreed about the central verities and doctrines of the faith, but they were dividing up in terms of strong and weak brethren, more enlightenment and less enlightenment. This again is an example of schism.

The great illustration, of course, in the church at Corinth arises out of the question of the spiritual gifts. Now one and the same Spirit had given gifts to these various people. They were given to the body and Christians were all meant to be uplifted and edified as the result of the exercise of these gifts. But instead of the gifts being a cause of unity and of edification their abuse had become a cause of division and of schism. In this matter also the Corinthian Christians were acting independently and were jealous and envious of one another.

Now those are the ways in which the apostle shows us exactly what is meant by this term 'schism': people who were agreed about the centralities of the faith dividing and separating from one another over matters that were not essential to salvation, not absolutely vital. This is always one of the dangers afflicting us as evangelicals. We can be too rigid. There is this kind of fissile tendency which has manifested itself frequently in the long history of the Christian church. This has always been the great charge brought against Protestantism by Roman Catholicism, and there is an element of truth in it. Martin Luther, led by the Spirit of God, made this great move, and he caused a division.

He separated; he went out; but the moment he did that, people began to separate from him. Soon there was the great division into Lutheran and Reformed, and then the Anabaptists in their various groups also came into being. The Roman Church said, That is it, the moment you leave us, this is what happens! And this has been a tendency among evangelicals.

I could give you some almost laughable illustrations of this. I hope I am not going to offend any national susceptibilities in what I am about to say, but the country that illustrates this particular point more clearly perhaps than any other is Scotland. There have been more divisions in the church in Scotland than in any other. They all tend to be Presbyterian, yet they are divided up into groups and denominations, and if you read their history, and particularly that of the eighteenth century, you will find differing groups which were known as the New Lights and the Old Lights, the Burghers and the Anti-burghers. Here were people who were agreed about the centralities of the faith, but they separated and formed separate churches over the question of whether or not you should take an oath to the borough to which you belonged.

Here I must tell you a rather amusing story vouched for as true. There was a minister in a certain church in Scotland, and he and his wife were very godly and very able people. But when the question of burgher subscription came in, the husband and the wife took different sides and held different views. It is said that when this good man and his wife left the manse on the first Sunday morning after their difference they walked together as usual until they came to the building where the husband ministered; but this morning, as the minister turned to the right to go into the church, instead of his wife turning with him, she continued on the road. And as she continued walking, she called to him and said, 'You may still be my husband but you are no longer my minister.' So she proceeded to go and worship with the Anti-burghers! Such is one of the dangers by which we are confronted. We can be so rigid, so over-strict, and so narrow that we become guilty of schism.

Now, there have been divisions among the Baptists and among the people called Brethren. The Plymouth Brethren started out by saying that they did not believe in any denominations. They were all brethren, they were all loving, but look at the history of that body, look at the divisions among them – and these, not on central matters of the faith, but very frequently on matters which are far from being central. Similarly there have been endless divisions among Baptists, Methodists, and various other denominations. Think of the position in the United States. Look at the number of denominations. Look at the divisions that have taken place among men who have held to the same evangelical faith. They have divided on personalities; they have divided on subtle, particular emphases. I believe that this is something that is also very true today in South Africa and in other parts of Africa. There is a multiplicity of denominations, and men do not hesitate to set themselves up and to start denominations – not in terms of vital truth but in terms of matters which are not even secondary, but of third-rate, fourth-rate, even perhaps twentieth- or hundredth-rate importance!

This, then, is one great danger that we have to keep in our minds as we try to define what we mean by 'evangelical'.

Succumbing to the Ecumenical Spirit

Then there is a second danger, and it is the exact opposite. It is the danger of being so broad, so wide, ana so loose that in the end we have no definitions at all. As I see things today, this is perhaps the greater danger because we are living in what is called an ecumenical age. People have reacted, and rightly, against the divisions in the past, these wrong and sinful divisions. But the danger is that you react so violently that you swing right to the other extreme and say that nothing matters except that we have a Christian spirit.

I believe that this is the danger which is tending to threaten us as evangelical Christians at this present time. And I must give you what I see as some of the ways in which this ecumenical tendency, this wrong and false ecumenical tendency, is tending to show itself. Certainly we must all believe in unity. Our Lord has established that once and for ever in His great high priestly prayer (John 17). It is everywhere in the New Testament. Our great endeavour should be to be one, yet this must not lead to a looseness in our thinking. We must not become subject to a false, vague, nebulous, ecumenical type of thinking. There are certain factors which seem to me to be promoting this danger and threatening our whole position, and I must mention them.

I believe that one of the most potent factors in this respect has been the Billy Graham campaigns. Let me explain what I mean by that. He has believed in the widest possible sponsorship, and his motive has been a good one. He is anxious to evangelize, and that is right; but whether it is equally right to be sponsored by people who in reality deny your very message is another matter. This is what he has tended to do; he has brought together people who previously had practically nothing to do with one another. I have seen this in several countries, but I remember hearing it very strikingly after his visit to Scotland. I met people who said, You know, we've discovered from the campaign that these other people, the Church of Scotland people and others whom we did not know and with whom we had nothing to do in the past, we've discovered they're very nice people, and we've had a very happy time working with them. This was very subtle, because they found that they were nice people – whether they had thought before that these people had horns and long tails I do not know – but the point was that they had been impressed by their niceness, by their friendliness, and by their brotherliness. This has had the effect of making these people take the next step and say, Well, I wonder whether these doctrines we've been emphasizing are so important after all. Isn't the great thing about us that we are Christians, that we've got this loving spirit, and that we're prepared to work together? I believe that in a very subtle way the Graham and other campaigns have had this kind of influence and have been shaking people's convictions as to what exactly it means to be evangelical.

Another extraordinary way in which it is happening is one with which I am familiar in England. There is a very real danger at the present time that if a man denounces liberalism in any respect, he is regarded as an evangelical. There are some advantages, you know, in being old, and one of them is that you do know just a little bit about history. I am old enough to remember the beginning of the Barthian movement and events surrounding it. There was a great old professor in Scotland, Donald Maclean. He and another man started a journal known as *The Evangelical Quarterly*, which is still in circulation. This was a truly evangelical periodical which was started to defend the Christian faith against the modernism and liberalism which were rampant in the 1920s. I will never forget meeting Professor Donald Maclean. He was one of the first men who ever mentioned the name of Karl Barth to me, and he spoke of him in the most lyrical terms, giving me the impression that Karl Barth was one of the greatest evangelicals who had ever lived. Why did Maclean do this? Well, because of Barth's onslaughts on the old liberalism. You see the subtlety of the thing. Because Barth was so wonderful a critic of liberalism he was regarded as a true evangelical, something that he, of course, never was.

Let me give you another example. There is a man who is regarded as a very great Christian and one of the great defenders of evangelicalism in England today, a journalist by the name of Malcolm Muggeridge. He is being used by evangelicals in their conferences and in their campaigns. An evangelical evangelist was going to hold a campaign last September for a month in London and one of the key men of the whole of the campaign was to be this man Malcolm Muggeridge. Why? Well, because Malcolm Muggeridge is a very wonderful critic of the Church of England, makes fun of bishops and so on, and is a radical critic of the mere show and pretence of what is called the establishment. Not only that, he is a person who undoubtedly has changed his position from having been a man of the world and a cynic to being one who now says that what is needed is the spirit of Christ, and he claims to be a Christian. Having read his last book, which is called *Jesus Rediscovered*, I would not hesitate to say that Malcolm Muggeridge is not a Christian at all. He does not believe in the virgin birth, he does not believe in the miracles as facts, he does not believe in the atonement, he does not believe in the literal physical resurrection, he does not believe in the person of the Holy Spirit, he does not believe in prayer, yet he is being used in evangelical conferences and meetings. Why? Only because he has changed his general position and is now talking vaguely about Christ. The man has actually become a mystic and he imposes his mystical views upon the Christian faith. But evangelicals in this age of looseness are ready to day hands suddenly upon any man who attacks the liberalism of the establishment and talks about Christ, without being careful to discover in detail what the man really believes.[1]

There have been many other examples of this. I find that C. S. Lewis has almost become the patron saint of evangelicals. He was never an evangelical and said so quite plainly himself. And I could give you many other illustrations and examples of the same thing.

Here then is a second factor which tends to produce this loose and vague idea, the ecumenical spirit that ultimately sells the pass and delivers us into a position in which we are no longer evangelical.

'The Holy Spirit, Not Doctrine'

Then there is a third factor which to me is a very serious one at the present time, and that is what is known as the charismatic movement. I am sure that you are all familiar with this. This is a phenomenon that has been confronting us for the last fifteen years or so, and it is very remarkable. It began in America and it has spread to many countries, most countries probably by now. Why am I referring to the charismatic movement under this heading? Because this again is something that has tended to undermine an insistence upon careful definition of our terms, and it does it in this way.

The teaching of this movement is that nothing matters except 'the baptism of the Spirit'. Sometimes they may put it

[1] Muggeridge subsequently joined the Roman Catholic Church.

in terms of speaking in tongues, but at any rate they put it in general terms of 'the baptism of the Spirit'. Nothing matters but this! I could give you several examples of this thinking. I read a book by one of the leaders in the movement, David Du Plessis, in which he actually states that theology does not matter, that what matters is this experience. Now one can understand in a measure what he means by this. He may have set out to say that a dull, theoretical, intellectual orthodoxy is of no value, and that the Christian must have life. That is true, but when he goes so far as to say that nothing matters but this experience and that theology does not count at all, he is contradicting the statements and the teaching of the New Testament, and he is putting himself into a very dangerous position.

Have you read the little book called *Catholic Pentecostalism*? If you have, you will have discovered the same thing there. This is the thesis of the book. It is a very clever book, but a very subtle and dangerous one from our evangelical standpoint. This is the argument: they say, Here we are, people belonging to different religious and cultural backgrounds, but we are all one because we have all had the baptism of the Spirit, and we are all speaking in tongues. They say, *this* is the thing that really matters. The book does not go on to say that you may need to change your doctrine. Indeed the author actually argues to the contrary. He says that the danger in the past has been that when people have received this baptism of the Spirit and have started speaking in tongues, they have left their churches and have joined the Pentecostal Church. Now, he says, this is quite wrong. Let me quote the book: 'Most Pentecostalists historically have come from amongst the Methodists. The Methodists have generally been an emotional and an unintellectual people.' And the result is that when they get this 'baptism of the Spirit', they manifest it and show it by a lot of hyper-emotionalism and excitement, and so on. Now that, he says, is all right, that is their cultural background; the Spirit comes to them in that cultural medium. But we are Catholics, Roman Catholics; we have got a great body of dogma and of doctrine; we have got our great history, our sacramental teaching, and our sacramental life. When we receive 'the baptism of the Spirit' we must not give up and shed all we have got, join the Pentecostals and simply take over their cultural background. That is quite unnecessary. We receive 'the baptism of the Spirit' in our cultural milieu, and the effect that it should have upon us is not to make us shed our doctrines and become Pentecostals. It should give us a deeper understanding and appreciation of our great heritage. Thus you find that these Roman Catholics, who claim to have had 'the baptism of the Spirit', all go on to testify that the main effect of their 'baptism of the Spirit' has been to increase their intimate knowledge of and communion with the virgin Mary. It has deepened their appreciation of the mass and all the other various Roman Catholic doctrines and dogma.

Now you can see the effect of all this. In the end it means that doctrine does not matter at all. You can believe Roman *charismatic movement* (handwritten)

Catholic doctrine, or be Methodist, or be without any doctrine at all if you like; it does not matter. The great thing is that you have this experience. And so they have their conferences and their congresses in which they all meet together, and they are virtually proclaiming that doctrine does not matter at all. Now this, you see, undermines the importance of arriving at definitions and descriptions of the faith. As this is coming into evangelical circles, and has come, it threatens our whole position as evangelical Christians and shows us the desperate urgency of re-examining the position and knowing exactly what we mean.

Then, to speak of England in particular, there has been a great change in the position of the evangelicals in connection with the Anglican Church. Now this is not a value judgment of mine on them; this is what they have said themselves. They had a conference in Keele in 1967 and produced a report, which you can read for yourselves. They condemned their own past; they condemned themselves for not taking a more active part in the Church of England. They condemned themselves for not being in the ecumenical movement and working actively in it, and they said this has been wrong and they have changed their policy. So now you find evangelical Anglicans taking an active part in the ecumenical movement, and they are as concerned as anybody else about church union with bodies that are not at all evangelical.

Here then is another factor which has tended to undermine the old understanding of the meaning of the word evangelical

the whole of christianity

and has undermined our confidence in what has been said in the past.

Non-Evangelical Opposition to Ecumenism

The last factor that I must mention to you is this: there are various denominations and church groupings that are opposed to the ecumenical movement but not on evangelical grounds. For instance, there are a number of men who are opposed to the ecumenical movement because the ecumenical movement postulates bishops as being essential to the united church. They know that in order to have a world church there must be an acceptance of bishops and a hierarchy; that is agreed by everybody. So there are now a number in all the denominations who on political and general ecclesiastical grounds say, We will never submit to bishops. They are therefore outside the ecumenical movement. And here is the problem: we are also outside the ecumenical movement. So they have tended to come to us and say that we are all one: we are not in this world church; we are out together in the wilderness, so do we not all belong together? We have had approaches from these people. As a matter of fact I had a personal experience of this which was quite amusing. A little book of mine was published and, to my amazement, it was reviewed by a well-known professor belonging to one of the English denominations. He praised my book to the skies; I could scarcely believe it. I thought that either he or I had gone mad, or perhaps both of us. However, the explanation of the favourable review was this: this man is anti-ecumenical because he does not believe in bishops, and so being now predisposed in my favour he picked up everything he could to praise in my book and said nothing about the rest. Here, you see, is a very subtle danger, the danger of our coming together to fight the ecumenical movement, but we must not do so. Why? Because these men are not evangelical. They are liberal. It is another reminder that we must be careful that we define our position carefully.

I close then, for the moment, by saying this. What has been said of the church in the past is true today. The church, though she has been reformed, must be constantly re-formed, *semper reformanda*. Always reform! The church is always to be under the word; she must be; we must keep her there. You must not assume that because the church started correctly, she will continue so. She did not do so in the New Testament times; she has not done so since. Without being constantly reformed by the word the church becomes something very different. We must always keep the church under the word, and we must keep a movement like the IFES under the word. *Semper reformanda*! And we have got to do this with the term evangelical. Every generation has got to examine this for itself. You cannot receive these things by tradition alone. This has always been the danger. People have said, I've been brought up as an evangelical; I am an evangelical. Are you? We have got to ask ourselves the question, and we must not be satisfied merely with definitions drawn up in the past because every age has had its own particular problems, and all the great confessions and creeds were generally drawn up to face some particular problem or situation. So it behoves us in our day and generation to examine this term evangelical anew and afresh in the light of the Scripture and of history, and especially in the light of the dangerous tendencies that surround us at this present time.

With this general introduction I leave our subject this morning. I hope to continue tomorrow and to put before you certain guiding principles which will enable us to arrive at an answer to the question, What is an evangelical in our day and generation? Let us pray:

O Lord our God, we come to thee again and we thank thee that we are found among thy people. We know that it is all of thy grace, that left to ourselves we would not only be out in the world but in the depth of sin and of iniquity. We thank thee that we are what we are by thy grace, and we thank thee that thou hast given us an interest in these things and a concern about them. O God, we are amazed that thou hast ever looked on us, and in a measure made us guardians and custodians of the faith. We pray thee, O Lord, to give us great wisdom and understanding, to give us great circumspection to enable us to walk carefully, for the times and the days are evil. Wilt thou continue therefore to look upon this conference and to brood upon it with thy Spirit, guiding every aspect of this work, and leading us all together to submit ourselves to thy most holy word and its divine instruction. Bless us, we pray thee, to that end and continue with us throughout the day. We ask it in the name of thy dear Son, our blessed Lord and Saviour, and the great Lord of the church, Jesus Christ. Amen.

II

I N yesterday's lecture, I was suggesting that we are in the same position as that in which Jude found himself. He had intended to give an exposition of the Christian faith in a broad and general manner, but owing to certain circumstances which had arisen, he had to abandon that and, instead, had to exhort these people to contend earnestly for the faith, once and for ever delivered to the saints.

My theme is that we are in a similar position today, and that it behoves us to examine the situation in which we now find ourselves and to make sure that we are clear in our minds as to what is meant by being an evangelical. We are not discussing, What is a Christian? but we are discussing, What is an evangelical? It is a limiting term, and I argued that we are in such a subtle situation that it is no longer sufficient that we subscribe to some general basis of faith. That is no longer enough; we have got to be more particular, because these changes, when they come in, though they generally insinuate themselves on the periphery of the faith, gradually spread further and further towards the centre.

We are familiar with the fact, and it is not something new, that people are prepared to subscribe to bases of faith or to creeds and, at the same time, make what we call mental reservations. This, in the end, means that they deny some of the most essential articles of these bases. This, again, makes it necessary for us to be particular and careful.

At the same time let us remember that we are not merely to define what is bare orthodoxy. You can have a dead orthodoxy. I am concerned to define the evangelical in a way which goes beyond statements of belief. It is as important to define the evangelical as being against a kind of Protestantism or even reformed scholasticism, as it is that we should define the evangelical by contrast with those who are heterodox in their doctrine and their belief.

Guiding Principles: (1) The Preservation of the Gospel

Let it also be understood that our object in this discussion should not be merely the preservation of a tradition. Traditions may be good, but when they become traditionalism, they are bad. We should not be concerned primarily with merely maintaining some recognized position or continuing in some particular tradition. That is not our object. Still less should we be concerned simply to be polemical or to have argument for the sake of argument.

Neither are we to be concerned for separation as such; indeed I would go further and say that our object should be, not to exclude people, but to include as many as possible, and yet to be careful that we are maintaining our principles and our landmarks.

I said yesterday, and repeat it again today, that the evangelical Christian should be very concerned about unity. He, of all men, should be concerned about the unity of the Spirit of truth and of peace, for this is part of his whole attitude and his whole outlook.

So our real reason for definition, and contending for this faith, is that we believe it to be vital to the preservation of the true gospel. That is why I am so concerned about bearing the historical element in our minds. History shows very clearly that when this emphasis is lost, the true gospel becomes lost sooner or later, and preaching also is lost and in vain, so that the church ceases to evangelize and to gain converts and adherents. *Attack opinion// be lied & then*

That then is our object. We are not concerned merely to be polemical, as I said, but our intent is a very practical one. We are concerned about the souls of men and women. We are here to spread the good news of salvation and to win people out of darkness into light. That is why we should be so careful about the truth, and always contend for it.

What, then, is to be our method in defining what an evangelical is? The method, of course, is primarily biblical. The great slogan of the Reformation, *sola scriptura*, has always been the slogan of the true evangelical. The evangelical starts with the Bible. He is a man of the Bible. He is a man of the Book. This is his only authority and he submits himself in everything to this. We will open this out later but we must assert it at the outset. This, you see, is already a differentiating point. Others start with philosophy, and with a more general principle, but the evangelical starts always with the Bible.

Guiding Principles: (2) Learning from History

Secondly, with reference to method, I am again concerned to emphasize that, at the same time, we must be historical in our approach. I know that it is very difficult for many modern people to realize this, but we are not the first people to have lived in this world. That needs to be said very frequently at the present time. There have been great generations of people and of Christians before us. Though we have split the atom, we are not very different from those who have lived in previous ages, so it is important that we should be guided by history. A man who has no respect for history is a fool, and he will soon discover that, when he finds himself repeating the errors of those who have gone before him.

We are concerned about history. At the same time we must not be bound by it; we must not be slaves to it. These are always the dangers that afflict us. Some people dismiss the whole of history. They are going to lave everything new and start everything afresh. We lave a world of movements. There are people in the universities at the present time who are more or less suggesting that you scrap the whole of the past, that you start anew and afresh in politics, in social and economic affairs, and in everything else. This same attitude tends to come into the religious realm, but we must exclude it.

At the same time it is equally important that we must recognize that nothing in this world has ever been complete, that while we thank God for the great events of the past, the great Reformation and other minor reformations, we must not be slaves to them. That is the way to develop a kind of scholasticism and an arid intellectualism.

So we pay respect to history, and we are prepared to learn from it, but we are not totally subservient to it in a wrong sense. That is the second guiding principle.

Guiding Principles: (3) Maintaining Negatives

The third is the importance of the place of negatives as well as positives. Now here, to me, is a tremendously important matter, and I am not sure that this is not going to be the most vital point in the dispute between evangelicals who are adhering to the old position and those who are tending to depart from it at the present time.

One of the first signs that a man is ceasing to be truly evangelical is that he ceases to be concerned about negatives, and keeps saying, We must always be positive. I will give you a striking example of this in a man whose name is familiar to most of you, and some of whose books you have read. This is what he has written recently: 'Whether a person is an evangelical is to be settled by reference to how he stands with respect to six points', which he then enumerates. His definition is by reference only to what a person is *for* rather than to what he is *against*. He goes on: 'What a man is, or is not, against may show him to be a muddled or negligent or inconsistent evangelical, but you may not deny his right to call himself an evangelical while he maintains these principles as the basis of his Christian position.'

Now that is the kind of statement which I would strongly contend against. I believe it is quite wrong. The argument which says that you must always be positive, that you must not define the man in terms of what he is against, as well as what he is for, misses the subtlety of the danger. If that argument is left uncontested the door is open to a repetition of such things as the Galatian heresy. You remember the Galatians and how the apostle has to deal with their heresy. It was the whole problem of Judaism, which emerges in several places in the New Testament. What was the Galatian heresy? Well, it stated that those people who had led the Galatians astray had not denied the gospel; they were not denying anything; what they were doing was to *add* something, namely circumcision, which, they said, was essential. Oh yes, they said, you've got to believe the gospel, all these positives are quite right. But then they brought in their addition. So it is important, you see, that the evangelical should also have his negative criticisms and be ready to say that you must *not* believe this and you must *not* do that.

History is helpful at this point also, and I will take an example that is most obvious to me. You have heard of Puritanism.

Puritanism was in England in the sixteenth century almost immediately after the Protestant Reformation. Puritanism was a section of Protestantism. The Reformation had come to England and the church had become Protestant. Who were these Puritans ? They were men who said that the Reformation had not proceeded far enough, that it had done its good work in connection with doctrine, but it had ceased to do it in connection with practice. They argued that this was inconsistent, that some practices, still allowed, were denials of the changed doctrine, and they wanted the Reformation to be carried through in the matter of practice as well as of doctrine.

The Puritans and the others in the Church of England were all agreed about the doctrine; the difference came in with regard to the negatives, and that is why these negatives are always of such great importance. So we shall have to be careful to maintain this observation on the place of negatives in our definition of evangelical.

Guiding Principles: (4) No Subtractions or Additions

A fourth general principle is this: that we must be very observant of people's *subtractions* from the truth on the one hand, and of their *additions* to the truth on the other.

I have discovered over the years that subtraction from the truth is something that members of churches are very, very slow to observe. I have almost come to the conclusion that the acid test to apply, to know whether a preacher is evangelical or not, is this: observe what he does not say! So often I have found that people have listened to a man and been carried away by him, and thought everything was wonderful, for the reason that he said nothing wrong, and they were quite right in their observation. The man had said nothing wrong, but the point was that he had not said certain things that an evangelical always must say; he had left them out.

I knew a minister who once went to listen to an American professor of theology called Nels Ferré. This minister was an evangelical but not a very well-instructed one. He listened to Nels Ferré and was completely carried away by him. He went back to his church and reported in lyrical terms on this marvellous address. What had happened? Well, what had happened was that Nels Ferré in that particular atmosphere had not said everything that he believed. All he had said then was perfectly right. He had not said anything specifically evangelical, neither had he, on that occasion, said anything of the heterodox thinking of which he was guilty.

There is no doubt that this question of subtracting from the truth, or leaving out part of the message, is a very vital one at the present time. You hear people talking about the Bible, and they can talk about the cross, but it is important to notice what they do *not* say about them. The fact that they mention them is insufficient. You must be careful in your observation of what a man does not say, as well as what he does.

Then, on the other hand, you have got to be careful about additions. I have already referred to them in dealing with the importance of negatives. Only recently I came across a striking example of this point. There is a certain bishop in England who is well known as an extreme Anglo-Catholic. He has recently become one of the chaplains of a certain shrine, the Shrine of our Lady of Walsingham in England. Although this man is now an extreme Anglo-Catholic, in his student days he was a thorough evangelical. As he was talking to a friend of mine who is an evangelical, he said: 'You know, I haven't ceased to believe anything I believed as a student. What I have done is to add on.'

Now many of us have said throughout the years that in some respects we have found ourselves nearer to the Roman Catholics than to the liberals because the Roman Catholics, after all, believe in the being of God, the deity of Christ, the virgin birth, the two natures of Christ in one person, the miracles, the atonement, the literal, physical resurrection, and the person of the Holy Spirit. On these truths we have always found ourselves in closer agreement; and sometimes we have found that by reading books by certain Roman Catholic authors our faith was strengthened because they believe what we believe, whereas the liberals and the modernists deny all this. I say this to illustrate the same point, that the trouble with the Roman Catholic is what he adds on and what he adds to or subtracts from what is stated in his belief.

So we must be careful, and remember the warning in the book of Revelation, where we are told we must not add to, or take from, anything that is written in that particular book, and the command belongs equally to all the other books of the Bible. We have got to keep our eye on these two sides: what men do not say, and what they add on, over and above what we regard as the true faith.

These are the general principles to guide us in our definition of what constitutes an evangelical, and I trust that I have already made it plain that this approach is essential because of the subtlety of the situation in which we find ourselves. If you merely take here the short list of desiderata and then ask an individual if he can accept them, and sign his name to the basis of faith, he may mislead you and mislead himself, because you have not asked him certain further questions. You have not observed what he has not said, or you have not discovered what he adds on to what you have in your basis of faith.

Using these guiding principles, let us then try to approach a definition of an evangelical. All I want to do at this point is to deal with his *general characteristics*. This is something we have not been doing so far, but I believe that the general characteristics of the evangelical are almost as important as the particular doctrines to which he subscribes. There is a kind of ethos which to me is of very great importance. I am coming increasingly to the opinion that the way in which a man thinks tells you as much about him as what he actually says. His whole method of thinking is one which is of supreme importance. So I would call attention here to certain general characteristics of the evangelical person.

Evangelical Priorities

First of all, the evangelical is one who is entirely subservient to the Bible. John Wesley said that he had become 'a man of one book'. This is true of every evangelical. He is a man of one book; he starts with it; he submits himself to it; this is his authority. He does not start from any extra-biblical authority. He confines himself and submits himself completely to the teaching of the Bible. I shall, of course, deal more fully with this when we come to details; I am now simply giving you the general characteristics.

The next thing about the evangelical is that he uses this term as a *prefix* and not as a suffix. Here again, I think this is something that is going to be increasingly important in the years to come. What I mean by that is that the *first* thing about the man is that he is evangelical. The particular denomination to which he belongs is secondary; it is not primary. In other words, there is all the difference in the world between talking about an evangelical Baptist and a Baptist evangelical. I am contending that our man is evangelical first. He may be a Baptist, he may be a Presbyterian, he may be Episcopalian, but he is primarily, first and foremost, evangelical.

Let me give you one illustration. There was a great controversy in England a few years ago as a result of the conference at Keele to which I referred yesterday. One man, who had been an archbishop in Australia, wrote a letter to the press in which he said that he was very willing to admit that he was an Anglican before being evangelical. His first, his fundamental, his ultimate loyalty was to Anglicanism, not to evangelicalism. He said, 'I am an evangelical, but I am an Anglican first.' I contend that when a man says that, he has already said something that makes him suspect as an evangelical. Evangelical first! Any other difference is something that should follow.

Watchfulness

Another characteristic of this evangelical is that he is a man who is *always watching*. Now all these things have to be said very carefully because there is a right and a wrong way to watch, but the evangelical is a man who is always watchful, and he is always watchful, of course, because the Scripture teaches him to be so.

'Watch and pray', says our Lord, and the apostle Paul, bidding farewell to the elders of the church at Ephesus, told them to do exactly the same thing. He warns them concerning the time following his departure: 'Take heed therefore unto yourselves, and to all the flock, over the which the Holy Ghost hath made you overseers, to feed the church of God… For I know this, that after my departing shall grievous wolves enter in among you, not sparing the flock' (Acts 20:28-29). So he exhorts them to be watchful.

Or again, take 1 Corinthians 16 where there is a striking statement of this same lesson to be found. The apostle, having gone through the great series of controversial matters which was tearing asunder the life of the church at Corinth, winds it up by saying: 'Watch ye, stand fast in the faith, quit you like men, be strong. Let all your things be done with charity' (1 Cor. 16:13-14). It is an exhortation to watch, to be careful. As Christians we are always in the midst of foes, 'For we wrestle not against flesh and blood, but against principalities and powers, against the rulers of the darkness of this world, against spiritual wickedness in high [or, heavenly] places' (Eph. 6:12).

The New Testament gives many examples of this. Paul in his exhortations to Timothy is constantly making the same point. He says in 1 Timothy 6:3-4: 'If any man teach otherwise, and consent not to wholesome words, even the words of our Lord Jesus Christ, and to the doctrine which is according to godliness; he is proud, knowing nothing, but doting about questions and strifes of words', and so on. The New Testament indeed is full of these exhortations to us, to watch and to be careful.

John comforts the Christians, confronted as they were, even then, by antichrists and false teachers, that they 'have an unction from the Holy One' (1 John 2:20) and that they are to exercise this. They are to be discriminating; they are always to be examining; they are always to be watchful. And so when a man ceases to be watchful, he, to that extent, ceases to be an evangelical. The person who says, It is all right; you need not bother; we are all Christians and having a marvellous time together – and is not watchful, is already departing from the biblical position.

Distrust of Reason

Then I come to another characteristic. This may very well be a highly controversial one, but in my estimate it is extremely important. It is, and I put it dogmatically and bluntly, that the evangelical *distrusts reason and particularly reason in the form of philosophy*. If you take a bird's-eye view of the history of the Christian church, this emerges very clearly indeed, and of course, the more you read of it in detail, the clearer it becomes. Every reformation has always expressed a distrust of reason and of philosophy. One of the earliest examples of this is to be found in Tertullian, one of the first great theologians of the Western church. He put it in a very striking form: 'What has Jerusalem to do with Athens? What has the temple to do with the porch and the academy?' He had, as you know, joined the Montanists, who were in rebellion against the tendencies to become subservient to Greek philosophy, that had come into the church.

I suggest to you that nothing is more important in our present situation than just this one particular point. Philosophy has always been the cause of the church going astray, for philosophy means, ultimately, a trusting to human reason and human understanding. The philosopher wants to encompass all truth; he wants to categorize and explain everything, and that is why there are no more important passages in the Scripture for us at the present time than the First Epistle to the Corinthians, starting in chapter i, at verse 17, and going right the way through to the end of chapter 4, with especial reference to chapter 2. The apostle's whole contention in those chapters is that things were going wrong in Corinth because they were beginning to bring back faith in human wisdom, philosophy; and his point is to show that this is diametrically opposed to the preaching of the gospel. He says he has become a fool for Christ's sake: 'If any man among you seemeth to be wise in this world, let him become a fool, that he may be wise' (1 Cor. 3:18). Here 'a fool' means that you do not trust to philosophy and to human wisdom. This is really a most important matter.

Martin Luther used to refer to 'that old witch, Lady Reason', and those of you who are familiar with his writings know how he constantly emphasized this point, that reason is an old witch. He was concerned about this, of course, because it was of the essence of his argument against Rome. It is true still that the trouble with Roman Catholicism is that they *say* that they believe the Bible. Let us grant that they do, and that they are quite sincere in saying that, but what, then, is the trouble? The trouble is that they have *added* Aristotelian philosophy on to their belief in the Bible, and that ultimately they are interpreting the Bible in terms of Aristotelian philosophy. That is the great characteristic of the *Summa* of Thomas Aquinas, and it was as the result of this that the evangel, the true gospel, had become entirely hidden. So it is not surprising that Luther should have contended so strongly against this very matter, and this is not, by any means, confined to Luther either.

I mentioned just now the Puritans in England, and they are a very good illustration of this same point. The great controversy between the Puritans and the Church of England was very largely an argument over the place of reason. There was a man called Richard Hooker, who, in many ways, determined what is called Anglicanism. Hooker introduced the term 'natural reason', and natural reason can determine how you govern your church and do many other things. This was the very essence of the argument between the Puritans, who were the true evangelicals, and these others in the Church of England, who, although they were Protestant, were not evangelical. It concerned this very matter of the place of reason.

We have got to be clear about what we mean by this because my statements can very easily be misunderstood. I base it all, as I said, on the teaching of 1 Corinthians 2 where Paul says: 'Now we have received, not the spirit of the world, but the spirit which is of God; that we might know the things that are freely given to us of God … But the natural man receiveth not the things of the Spirit of God: for they are foolishness unto him: neither can he know them, because they are spiritually discerned' (verses 12, 14). These are things which are revealed to us and which the Spirit alone can enable us to receive. 'He that is spiritual judgeth all things, yet he himself is judged of no man' (verse 15). I am also thinking of the words of our Lord as quoted in Matthew 11:25-26: 'I thank thee, O Father, Lord of heaven and earth, because thou hast hid these things from the wise and prudent, and hast revealed them unto babes. Even so, Father: for so it seemed good in thy sight.'

Such is the basis for the evangelical's distrust of human reason, and, as I say, trace the history of the church and you will find that a failure to recognize danger in this area has been the problem all along. You see, when the apostles died, the whole question of authority arose in the church. Not only that, the church was being persecuted, and in the second century there arose a number of men in the church called apologists, some of whom had been trained as Greek philosophers. They were concerned to show that there was no contradiction between the gospel and Greek philosophy. Their motive no doubt was a very good one, but I suggest to you that in doing this they compromised the gospel, they turned it into a philosophy, and they lost something vital in the realm of the Spirit. The church eventually became institutionalized and this led to the Roman Catholicism of the Middle Ages, the period prior to the Protestant Reformation.

This tendency has kept on recurring, and that is why I think it is so important for us, because I believe it is happening again now. Let me state it still more bluntly by putting it to you like this, that the true evangelical is not only distrustful of reason, but he is also distrustful of scholarship. Here we are, belonging to IFES, students and members of universities, and I am saying that the evangelical is distrustful of scholarship, and I maintain that! What do I mean? Let me try to make it plain. The evangelical starts from the Scriptures. He also reads the history of the church, and there he finds that the history proves what has been emphasized in the Scripture, that when men trust to reason and to understanding they go astray. He also finds that the men whom God has had to raise up and to use to call back people to the faith have often been very simple men. Not always, of course – I mentioned Luther and others, and I could have mentioned Calvin – but so often this has happened, that the revival in the church and the calling back of the people to the true faith has been done through the medium of someone quite unknown.

The sum of all I am saying is that the evangelical distrusts scholarship and is watchful of it. That does not mean that he is anti-intellectual; it does not mean that he becomes obscurantist; but it does mean that he keeps reason and scholarship in their place. They are *servants* and not masters.

The Place of Reason

What then is the place of reason in our faith and in our Christian life? I would define it like this. Reason must never determine *what* we believe. The business of reason is to teach us *how* to believe. It is an instrument, and the trouble arises always when people allow reason to determine what they believe. In other words, instead of submitting themselves to the Scripture, they turn to science, to philosophy, or to one of a number of other disciplines, and their position is determined by these things. They allow reason to determine what they believe instead of how they believe and how they think. Not *what* you think, but *how* you think, that is the place of reason, and I would say exactly the same thing about scholarship.

Now I am old enough to remember a generation of evangelicals who would have nothing at all to do with scholarship. Their attitude was, 'Scholarship is a menace and a danger; have nothing to do with it!' I knew men who were old when I was comparatively young who used to advise students for the ministry not to study theology. I recall one well-known evangelical leader who always used to tell such men, 'Whatever else you study at Oxford or Cambridge, don't study theology or you'll lose your faith.' That is something which I do not commend. I would condemn that attitude. That is the spirit of fear, and it leads to an obscurantism where you bury your head in the sand, and you are not aware of what is happening.

My contention is that the evangelical, while he realizes the danger of reason and scholarship, is not afraid of them. He does not run and hide, and just turn in on himself and the enjoyment of his own feelings. No, he is aware of scholarship, he meets it on its own level, but he does not submit himself to it. He does not go down on his knees because some man is a great scholar. He knows that the great scholar, even the great scholar in the Bible, may be an unbeliever, so he does not worship the scholar. It is when men begin to bow the knee to scholarship, submit themselves to it, almost worship it, and to regard it as the ultimate authority, that I suggest they have sold the pass and ceased to be truly evangelical.

The evangelical is not a bit afraid of scholarship. There is no need for us to be afraid of scholars if they are not Christians because they base their position on reason, and it is a simple matter to debate with them because they do not know the Scriptures. You can easily show them that what they have been saying they have spun out of their own minds. It is human reason, speculation, and philosophy, and not the true Christian teaching. The big principle that I would lay down is this, that in the attitude of the evangelical to reason and scholarship he is fully aware of the danger for he sees it so clearly in the Scripture. Paul becomes 'a fool', laughed at by the philosophers. They regarded his teaching as utter foolishness. This has always happened to the true Christian; it happens today. It is not surprising that the so-called great philosophers are sceptics and infidels. We should expect them to be, and we should not be frightened because they are. We should not apologize for the faith because they are not Christian. Rather we should see that this is a proof of the teaching of the Scripture; and we remember that when the church has gone down into the trough, in her deadest periods, it has invariably been when she has become subservient to philosophy.

Coming to more recent times, and to our own times, is it not a simple fact to say that the real damage to the life of the church in the last two centuries has been done mainly by theological seminaries? Is not that where the trouble has arisen? It has not arisen in the churches. It has arisen in the theological seminaries. Men who have felt called to the ministry and been recommended by churches for ministerial training have gone into the seminaries as evangelicals and true evangelists, and they have come out denying everything, sometimes even departing from the faith altogether. If that has not happened, they have come out dead, trying to be scholars and having lost the edge of their zeal and their enthusiasm. They are no longer truly presenting the truth. These are sheer facts.

Therefore, if an evangelical is not distrustful of reason and of scholarship, he is not only failing to understand the teaching of the Scripture; he is blind to this clear testimony of the history of the Christian church throughout the centuries. Why I am elaborating and emphasizing this is because the movements to which I referred yesterday, the 'new evangelicalism', and so on, are concerned with scholarship, in my opinion, in the wrong sense. This is a part of evangelicalism's inferiority complex. We want to be considered intellectual and respectable, and in doing that we are in grave danger of submitting ourselves to philosophy, to reason, and to scholarship, and it will lead to the same result with us as it has in the case of those who have gone before us.

Other Marks of an Evangelical

The next thing about the evangelical is that he *takes a particular view with regard to the sacraments*. I am not going to open this out this morning; I am hoping to do so tomorrow. The evangelical, speaking broadly, always takes a 'low' view of the sacraments. He recognizes only two, of course, like other Protestants, but his view of these often differentiates him, and generally does differentiate him, from those who are not evangelical.

The next point which I would make is that the evangelical *takes a critical view of history and tradition.* I have already emphasized that he pays attention to it, and great attention, and yet he is critical. The evangelical position, you see, is really always on a knife-edge. You have the two sides, two dangers, and the evangelical is here on this knife-edge between them. Let me put it in these terms: the evangelical emphasizes the principle of discontinuity rather than of continuity. Roman Catholicism obviously emphasizes the principle of continuity, tradition. So do most of the major denominations. I know it would be very interesting if I began examining you one by one this morning, and asked you why you belong to the denomination to which you belong. You would find almost invariably that it is an accident, that you did not decide it for yourself. Some of you have, perhaps, but not the majority. Most people are Baptists, Presbyterians, Methodists, whatever they are, simply because their parents were. They have been brought up in it. They are governed entirely by tradition. And you will find good people who, the moment you suggest that there is anything wrong with their denomination, can flare up, lose their tempers, and defend it to the last ditch, though they really know very little about it. Why? Because they are tied by this principle of tradition. And the idea of leaving their denomination is, to them, the greatest of all sins!

Now this is not evangelical. The evangelical believes in the principle of discontinuity. Looking at the history of the church, he sees how the church, which was a live, spiritual body, always tended to become hardened and fossilized into a dead institution. He realizes that this is the greatest danger, so, far from being afraid of the principle of discontinuity, he knows that he can only understand the true history of the living church in terms of discontinuity, the breaks that have taken place before the Reformation, and particularly at the Reformation, and since the Reformation.

In the same way, I could illustrate freely from the teaching of the Protestant fathers and others, that the evangelical is not tied by the decisions of early councils in the church. He does not slavishly fall down before them. He examines them, he examines everything in the light of the Scriptures, even the great pronouncements of the councils and everything else.

This leads me to the next thing, which is that an evangelical is a man who is *always ready to act on his beliefs*. I would say that this is a very striking characteristic of the evangelical. There are other people who are prepared to argue and discuss and even change their opinion, but they do not do anything about it. The evangelical, however, is a man who acts on his convictions. There would never have been Protestantism if this were not true.

Luther acted on what he came to see from the Scriptures, so did Calvin and Knox: all these men have done the same. And this, to me, is a very vital thing about the evangelical. He is not a theorist, he is not a theoretician; he is a living soul, he is a man who has got the Spirit in him, and he wants to act on what he believes. He is not afraid to change, and, of course, as I have already shown, it is because of this principle that bis danger is to become guilty of schism. For, while I say that he distrusts reason, he does have a faculty of reason, and he uses it; he studies the Scriptures; he discovers the doctrine and he can judge that it is true and can see that the people with whom he is connected do not believe it. He says, I cannot go on like this, I am compromising my doctrine; I have got to act on the truth. That is the evangelical. But, as I say, his danger is to overdo this and to become guilty of schism. Nevertheless, he is a man who is ready to change and ready to act on his belief, and this is something that differentiates him from people who are not evangelical.

Let me come to the next principle which is this, *the evangelical is a man who always simplifies everything*. Everything becomes simple. This is a great characteristic of the evangelical. Contrast what the evangelical believes with all that a Roman Catholic is asked to believe, and you will see how the Reformation simplified belief. The reformers started with what they called the 'perspicuity', the clarity, of the Scriptures. Rome had made faith difficult and involved, as the Pharisees had made the Jewish law involved with their glosses upon it and their multitude of explanations. Religion became a great mass of instruction with authorities which had to be quoted to show your learning.

The effect of becoming evangelical is always to simplify and to make things clear. The evangelical is a clear thinker. The Catholic is never a clear thinker; he is involved, he is difficult, he is subtle. You find great trouble in following him because of his involved method of argumentation. Philosophy is difficult, but the gospel, by contrast, is essentially simple.

The gospel not only simplifies belief and the statement of beliefs; it always simplifies our view of church order and church government. This is an essential evangelical characteristic. The Roman Catholic line of thinking always has its hierarchies. Church government is always involved. The more evangelical a man is, the simpler will be his church order and his idea of church government.

The same applies to his idea of worship. Evangelical worship is always simple by contrast with other forms. The evangelical does not believe in vestments, putting on copes and mitres and changing vestments for different parts of the service. He does not believe in ceremonies and liturgies and processions. He dislikes formalism. He believes in freedom, the freedom of the Spirit. This is the essential characteristic. When the Spirit is lost, and the man ceases to be evangelical, you will find that he will always elaborate his service, he will bring in additions to his appearance, his clothing, and to what he does.

Formalism is the characteristic of the non-evangelical; freedom is the characteristic of the evangelical.

Indeed, this principle of simplicity is one that I could show you very clearly from the history of the church, even with respect to buildings. The church buildings of the evangelical are always simple, whereas those of the Catholics tend to be ornate and elaborate. This principle of simplification is one that emerges in the total life of the evangelical.

The next point which I hurry on to is that the evangelical is *always concerned about the doctrine of the church*. Now I am in some difficulty at this point because it has always been my criticism of the IVF in Britain and every similar movement in other parts of the world, that we have not paid sufficient attention to the doctrine of the church, and to that extent we have not been as evangelical as we should be. The evangelical throughout the centuries has been very concerned about the doctrine of the church. That is usually why he has left different sections of the church, or different bodies, or denominations. He is concerned about a pure church. His idea of the church is that it consists of the gathered saints. He does not believe in a state church. He is vitally concerned about his correct view of the nature of the Christian church. One can see very clearly in the history of the church that the great fight throughout the centuries has been the fight between institutionalism and a living body of believing people. The doctrine of the church, then, is a very vital one. I am sorry but I cannot digress further on this matter now. I merely bring it to your attention for the time being.

Uppermost Concerns

The next thing, clearly, about the evangelical is *the tremendous emphasis that he puts upon the rebirth*. This is absolutely basic to him; he is not interested in dead orthodoxy, he is not interested in Protestant scholasticism. This is to me a very important differentiating point at the present time. The evangelical is a man who emphasizes the rebirth: a new beginning, born of the Spirit, new life in Christ, and partakers of the divine nature. I need not emphasize this here, I am sure, but you will find that as men cease to be evangelical, they put less and less emphasis upon regeneration, and they tend to put more and more upon the activity of the human will and the decision of the individual person. But the evangelical sees everything in terms of regeneration, the action of God. He says, I am what I am by the grace of God; and he is amazed at himself. This is the characteristic evangelical, but let me add to this.

The evangelical, because of this, is not merely interested in the need for life and power, he emphasizes it with the whole of his being. Take the question of pietism. Pietism has almost become a pejorative term at the present time and a term of abuse. I am getting very tired of evangelicals attacking pietism. I maintain that the true evangelical is always pietistic and it is the thing that differentiates him from a dead orthodoxy. I referred earlier to the origins of pietism on the continent of Europe. Arndt, Spener, and Francke, and people who followed them – this pietistic movement – arose as a protest, because, unfortunately, within a hundred years of the Protestant Reformation, both the Lutherans and the Reformed people had settled down into a dead orthodoxy. The same recovery happened in England under a man called William Perkins. Calvin himself was known and described as a theologian of the Spirit, and that is right. In true evangelicals, as you find in the Puritans and in a man like Jonathan Edwards in America, the pietistic element is very prominent in their teaching, and it always must be. The evangelical is not *merely* an orthodox man. You can have men who are quite orthodox but who are dead, and you really do not feel you can have any fellowship with them; their religion is all intellectual. Now that is not evangelicalism.

The evangelical has a true and a correct evangelical belief, but he does not stop at that. He has this great emphasis upon life, so you will always find in evangelical circles that there is great emphasis on the study of the Bible, personal and corporate, that great attention is paid to expositions of the Scripture and to prayer. Prayer is vital in the life of the evangelical.

Even in connection with this movement, the IFES, I have known men from certain countries who have been utterly, entirely orthodox, but the churches to which they belonged not only did not have prayer meetings, but they did not believe in prayer meetings. You could not wish for anything better from the standpoint of orthodoxy, but they do not believe in prayer meetings. Prayer has very little place in their lives. Now while they may be orthodox, I take leave to suggest that they are not truly evangelical. This element of prayer is essential to the evangelical; it is his life; it is vital to him. You will find that evangelicals almost invariably have formed religious societies for reading the Bible, discussing it together, for prayer, and for sharing one another's experiences. You had these things in pietism on the Continent and among the Puritans in England; you had it in the class meetings of the Methodists and in the societies that came into being in the eighteenth century. This is the great characteristic of evangelicalism.

Not only that. Evangelicals pay great attention to the way in which people live. They are strict in their behaviour. This used to be one of the most prominent characteristics of evangelicalism. I remember in my first contacts with the student movement, the people of the SCM and others used to describe those who belonged to the evangelical unions, the evangelicals, in these terms, Ah, they're the people who don't go to cinemas, they don't drink, and they don't smoke. I do not think they say that about them now. There has been a great change, but I am one of those who believe that there was a great deal to be said for the old position. The evangelical is careful about his life, careful to maintain good works, to live a life above reproach, not to be a hindrance or an obstacle to a weaker brother. The great ethic, the emphasis on holiness of the New Testament, is something which true evangelicals have always set great store by. They were called Puritans for that reason; they were called Methodists because they were methodical and careful. They did not merely content themselves with an intellectual belief. No, their whole life had to be governed by their doctrine. 'Every man that hath this hope in him purifieth himself, even as he is pure' (1 John 3:3). The emphasis on holiness in personal life and in church life is a great characteristic of evangelicalism.

Yet another characteristic is *the evangelical's interest in revival.* The only people who are ever interested in revival are evangelicals, and a good way of testing the quality of a man's evangelicalism is his interest in revival. The institutional people do not often talk about revival. They try sometimes to pay lip-service to it but they do not believe in it. They are governed by their ecclesiology and so on. The true evangelical, on the other hand, is always longing for an outpouring of the Spirit, and the great evangelical reawakenings have always been a result of an effusion of the Holy Spirit. The evangelical by nature is tremendously interested in revival.

Then, of course, the evangelical *always gives primacy to preaching.* When people cease to be interested in preaching, they cease to be evangelical. If you put discussions before preaching you are beginning to deny your evangelicalism. The church starts with preaching. Revivals, reformations, have always been great restorations of preaching. To the evangelical, nothing compares with preaching. Even reading is very secondary to preaching – 'truth mediated through personality', the impact of a man filled with the Spirit proclaiming the message of God!

My last point is that the evangelical is a man who is *always concerned about evangelism*. There are people who are orthodox, but who are not concerned about evangelism. To that extent they are not evangelical. The evangelical is a man who, because of what God has done for him, is anxious that others should have the same. Not only that, he sees something of the glory and the majesty and the sovereignty of God; he believes in hell, eternal punishment; and he is concerned about those men dying in spiritual darkness round and about him. They become a burden to him, and he is not satisfied until he has done his utmost to bring them to the knowledge of the truth as it is in Christ Jesus.

There, rather too hurriedly, I have tried to give you a general picture of the character of an evangelical person. In the next lecture I hope to consider what he believes in more detail. Let us pray:

O Lord our God, we again come unto thee, and we are increasingly amazed, O Lord, that thou hast ever looked upon us and entrusted these matters to us. God have mercy upon us. We humbly pray thee to look upon us and to speak to us through thy word. Send thy Spirit upon it and upon us. Give us, O God, this living and live concern. Awaken us, O Lord, to the dangers of the hour in which we live, in the perils of this modern situation. Lord, keep us humble, keep us from a hypocritical spirit, but give us a single eye to thy glory and to thy praise, and then an interest in, and a concern for, the souls of men and women. Continue, O Lord, among us this day in thy benediction and in thy grace. We ask it in the name of Jesus Christ, our Lord. Amen.

III

I HAVE been arguing that the great call that comes to us at this present time is that we should contend earnestly for the faith. Or, if you prefer it in the words of the apostle Paul, we must 'stand fast in one spirit, with one mind striving together for the faith of the gospel' (Phil. 1:27). We have considered reasons why, owing to certain tendencies which have arisen and certain statements which have been made, it has become essential for us once more to define exactly what we mean by an evangelical. What we could assume even ten years ago, we can no longer assume. Subtle changes are taking place as I described in the first lecture, and these compel us to ask again the question, What is an evangelical?

Yesterday we took a general view of the evangelical person, and I attach great importance and significance to the general view. A man's whole way of thinking, his outlook, sometimes tells us as much about him as what he tells us in detail. At times, indeed, it tells us even more.

We can now proceed to greater detail and ask what it is in particular that we desiderate in an evangelical, and what it is that an evangelical must believe. Obviously, as the centuries demonstrate so clearly, this is not an easy matter, but we must attempt it. Our primary concern, I would remind you once more, should not be to be exclusive. We must be as *inclusive* as we can and yet draw certain lines which we regard as being essential.

It can be taken for granted that we all agree that we must subscribe to a doctrinal basis such as that found in the constitution of the IFES. When this basis was drawn up, the object was to state things which we regarded, and still regard, as being essential and vital. You cannot read this doctrinal basis, however, without noticing that there are many doctrines in connection with the Christian faith that are not mentioned at all. These omissions raise the problem which we must consider.

Foundational and Secondary Truths

We clearly regard certain truths as being essential; there are others which, while we would say that they are important, and very important, we would not lay down as being *essential*. What we have to do, therefore, is to draw a basic distinction between truths and doctrines which we insist are essential or foundational, and others concerning which there can be a legitimate difference of opinion.

I am going to start with those truths which we regard as being essential; but my whole emphasis, and the case I am trying to present to you, is that it is not sufficient any longer merely to take these statements as they are. We have to elaborate them, we have to define them in greater detail, and we have to do this because of recent changes, and because we are confronted by the phenomenon of people subscribing to a basis of faith with what they call mental reservations. In view of that we are entitled to put certain questions to people, or if you like, we are entitled and compelled to define our statements in somewhat greater detail.

So what I am going to do is to assume these basic doctrines that are stated here in this basis, with which, I take it, you are all familiar, but I am going to draw out certain of these truths more particularly in the light of the present situation. In doing this, I am simply trying to do what has been done by our forefathers.

Take any confession of faith that has ever been drawn up in the past. You will always find that in addition to making statements of the truth as believed by truly Christian people, they have in addition gone beyond that, and they have defined these truths in the light of certain problems and circumstances that obtained at that time, in their day and generation.

For instance, it is obvious that in the Augsburg Confession, and in various other original Protestant confessions, the authors were deliberately expounding their positive belief in the light of erroneous Roman Catholic belief. This is always necessary. Take the earlier creeds, the Athanasian Creed and others. These were obviously written and elaborated, not merely to make positive statements of the faith, but to counteract certain heresies that had arisen at that time, such as the Arian heresy and others.

Now I suggest that we have got to do the same thing. That is why I have been asserting that we must not merely slavishly adopt, subscribe to, and continue to defend, the confessions and the creeds that have come down to us. We must go beyond that and show the relevance of these statements to our own day and generation.

Justifying a Vital Distinction

I am now going to do that, and I will also have to do a second thing, namely, to justify this distinction between doctrines that are essential (on which we must insist), and other doctrines which, while we regard them as true, we do not describe as being essential, and to differentiate between them. You can see why the need for this arises. The moment you state the basic and essential truths, you divide yourself off from people who are heterodox or who have virtually no belief at all, who merely say, perhaps, that they believe in God, while they do not even define what they mean by that. The moment you do this, you are confronted by a further problem. Having separated yourself from unbelievers, or from false professors of the Christian faith, you are now confronted by the problem of maintaining unity among yourselves. As I have tried to show, when people take doctrine seriously, a tendency develops in them, not perhaps to take it too seriously, but to become so particular and rigid that they demand too much, and put into the category of essential what should be regarded rather as non-essential. We have got to be careful that we do not fall into that error. While we must elaborate the meaning of essential truths even though it may cause division, it is also very right that we should establish this distinction between things which are essential and things which are not essential. If evangelicals do not do this, we shall be atomized and divided up in such a manner that we shall cease to count and cease to bear a corporate witness in this needy modern world.

This is a very old distinction which I am drawing between the essentials and the non-essentials. Let me give it to you in the words of Calvin in the *Institutes*, Book 4, Chapter 1, Section 12, where he puts it very clearly:

> For not all the articles of true doctrine are of the same sort. Some are so necessary to know that they should be certain and unquestioned by all men as the proper principles of religion. Such are: God is one; Christ is God and the Son of God; our salvation rests in God's mercy; and the like. Among the churches there are other articles of doctrine disputed which still do not break the unity of faith. Suppose that one church believes – short of unbridled contention and opinionated stubbornness – that souls upon leaving bodies fly to heaven; while another, not daring to define the place, is convinced nevertheless that they live to the Lord. What churches would disagree on this one point? Here are the apostle's words: 'Let us therefore, as many as are perfect, be of the same mind; and if you be differently minded in anything, God shall reveal this also to you' (Phil. 3:15). Does this not sufficiently indicate that a difference of opinion over these nonessential matters should in no wise be the basis of schism among Christians?

First and foremost, we should agree on all points. But since all men are somewhat beclouded with ignorance, either we must leave no church remaining, or we must condone delusion in those matters which can go unknown without harm to the sum of religion and without loss of salvation.

But here I would not support even the slightest errors with the thought of fostering them through flattery and connivance. But I say we must not thoughtlessly forsake the church because of any petty dissensions. For in it alone is kept safe and uncorrupted that doctrine in which piety stands sound and the use of the sacraments ordained by the Lord is guarded.[1]

That, I think, is a very perfect statement of the position which I am trying to put before you. So, with that introduction, and bearing in mind the danger of going to the wrong extreme of laxity, looseness, and indifferentism on the one hand, and over-rigidity and too much particularity on the other, let us proceed to this task.

The first thing that I am anxious to do is to make some comments on these things which we agree are essential. I am saying that we have got to elaborate somewhat upon what we stte here in this basis of faith. Indeed, I venture to suggest that we might even add something which will help to clarify the current situation.

---

[1] John Calvin, *Institutes of the Christian Religion*, trans. F. L. Battles, ed. J. T. McNeill, vol. 2 (Philadelphia: Westminster Press, 1960), pp. 1025-26.

The Necessity of Opposition to Doctrinal Indifferentism

In the light of the position in which we find ourselves I suggest that it would be a very good thing for us to state plainly and clearly that we are anti-ecumenical. Why do I start with a negative like this? For the reason that today we have to assert and defend the position that *doctrine is really vital and essential.* The ecumenical movement, while paying lip-service to a very minimum amount of credal statement, is merely based on doctrinal indifferentism. I think that this is generally agreed. You cannot have an ecumenical movement of the contemporary kind without such indifferentism. Even if ecumenists try to claim that they have a general subscription to a belief in Jesus Christ as God and Saviour, according to the witness of the Scriptures, we cannot regard this as sufficient, because they refuse to test subscription among themselves. In other words, they refuse any element of discipline, and this, it seems to me, is immediately something which proclaims indifferentism. There is no purpose in having a credal test unless you insist upon it, and unless you test people's subscription to it. We cannot admit this category of 'mental reservation'. Indeed, we are driven to say this by the notorious fact that there are men in the ecumenical movement who, in their own books and articles and statements, clearly show that they deny what we would regard as many of the essentials of the Christian faith.

There are men prominent in that movement, about whom it is doubtful whether they are even theists. It is not what I

69

am saying about them; it is what they themselves say in their books, and we are all familiar with these facts.

Therefore we start by asserting the vital importance of doctrine, and of being clear with regard to our doctrine and belief, and so we have no fellowship with those who do not insist upon the centrality of doctrine. Though it sounds a negative point, it is ultimately a very positive one. Clearly we have nothing in common with people who do not insist in this way upon clear statements of doctrine and of truth.

Having said that, we now go on to deal with some of the particulars that are mentioned in our agreed basis of faith. I have to make specific comments on some of them.

Scripture: The Only and Full Authority

The first is the doctrine of Scripture. The basis of faith says: 'We believe in the divine inspiration and entire trustworthiness of holy Scripture as originally given, and its supreme authority in all matters of faith and conduct.' I contend that it is not enough just to say that; we have got to go further. There are people who claim to subscribe to that doctrine, who, I would suggest, in some of their statements raise very serious doubts as to whether they really do accept it.

So we have to say some specific things such as that the Scripture is our *sole* authority, not only the 'supreme' authority, but our sole authority, our only authority. I say this to emphasize that we do not accept tradition as an authority in any sense of that term. We reject the Roman Catholic teaching with regard to tradition which is, as you know, that tradition is equal in authority with the Scriptures. Roman Catholics do not deny the authority of the Scriptures, but they give to tradition, the tradition elaborated in and by the church, an equal authority with the Scriptures. And in that tradition they would claim to have received revelation subsequent to the end of the New Testament canon.

We reject that, but we also reject another view of tradition which is much more subtle and much more dangerous, and which, one observes with great regret, has been creeping into the minds of some evangelical people in these last few years. What is this other idea of tradition? Well, it was a point of view first elaborated by John Henry Newman in the last century. Newman wrote a book dealing with the development of doctrine in the church. And he put it like this, that we must not say that the church has received new revelation, rather that the church through her experience and understanding, as the centuries passed, has been able to discover what was before only implicit in the Scriptures, and has been able to draw it out. This is the new and more subtle form in which the idea of tradition is being reintroduced and given great prominence.

This is the way in which men can justify certain practices such as episcopacy and so on, and still claim to be guided by the Scripture. They say it is right and true to say that episcopacy is not actually taught as such in the Scripture, but it is there 'implicitly', and the mind and the experience of the church has been led by the Holy Spirit to draw it out, to discover it, and to spell out its meaning. In this way you have tradition coming in, not perhaps as an equal authority, but as a very important one, and one which justifies certain other beliefs and practices. I suggest that we must emphasize that the Scripture is our *sole* authority, and that with respect to authority we cannot give any place to tradition in any shape or form.

Certainly evangelicals say that we can learn from the expositions of Scripture by the fathers throughout the centuries, but we do not regard these sources as authoritative in any sense whatsoever.

Furthermore it seems to me that we have got to spell out much more clearly the whole notion of revelation. It is difficult to do that in a short statement. The basis speaks of 'the divine inspiration and entire trustworthiness', but we must go beyond that. We have got to assert today this category of revelation. We have got to exclude the notion that men have arrived at the truth as a result of searching and thinking, or by means of philosophy. We must affirm that it is entirely given, that 'holy men of God spake as they were moved by the Holy Ghost' (2 Pet. 1:21), or, as Paul is constantly reminding his readers, that his gospel is not his own, 'For I neither received it of man, neither was I taught it, but by the revelation of Jesus Christ' (Gal. 1:12). We have to underline in a new and very definite way the whole notion of revelation and also, in the same way, of inspiration, showing that by inspiration we do not mean that these men were inspired in the way that certain poets have been 'inspired' and given glimpses into truth, but that they were actually controlled by the Holy Spirit. 'Borne along', as Peter writes in 2 Peter 1:21, or as Paul puts it in 2 Timothy 3:16: 'All scripture is given by inspiration of God'; it is 'God-breathed'. These things we must assert with particularity.

In the same way we have got to assert today that we believe that Scripture contains propositional truth. This has often been the dividing line between evangelicals and pseudo-evangelicals. I have noticed over the years that it is one of the first points that indicates a departure from an evangelical position when men begin to object to, and to reject, propositional truth, as Karl Barth did and as most of his followers still do. But we claim that in the Bible there are propositions, truths stated in propositional form, with regard to God and His being and His character, and many other matters. We have got to assert this element of propositional truth.

Likewise we have to assert particularly the supernatural element in the Scripture. What do I mean? Well, we have got to emphasize that we believe in prophecy in the sense of foretelling. The emphasis today is on 'forthtelling'. We admit that we agree that prophecy is forthtelling but, over and above that, it is foretelling. To me one of the profoundest arguments for the unique inspiration of the Scriptures is the truth of prophecy, the fulfilment of prophecy. We have got to emphasize this extraordinary manifestation of the supernatural.

We have also to insist upon a belief in the literal truth and historicity of the miracles of the Old and the New Testament, because there are people who say that they can still subscribe to our general statement about the inspiration and the authority of the Scriptures, who increasingly are denying the historicity of many of the Old Testament miracles, and indeed are trying to explain away some of the New Testament miracles in terms of science or psychology. We must assert the historicity of these manifestations of the supernatural.

Then the next thing to be said under this heading of Scripture is that we must believe the whole Bible. We must believe the history of the Bible as well as its didactic teaching. Failure here is always an indication of a departure from the true evangelical position. Today there are men who say, Oh yes, we believe in the Bible and its supreme authority in matters of religion, but, of course, we don't go to the Bible for science; we go to it for help for our souls, for salvation and help and instruction in the way to live the Christian life. They are saying that there are, as it were, two great authorities and two means of revelation: one of them is Scripture and the other is nature. These, they say, are complementary, they are collateral, and so you go to the Scriptures for matters concerning your soul, but you do not go to them to seek God's other revelation of himself in nature. For that, you go to science.

You are familiar with this view which, it seems to me, is not only extremely dangerous, but tends to undermine our whole position. We have got to contest it, and contest it very strongly. There is one thing about this present tendency which is quite amazing to me, and it is that those who advocate it seem to think that they are saying something quite new; but it is not new. It is precisely what Ritschl and his followers were teaching a hundred years ago. 'Judgments of fact' and 'judgments of value', as they called them. It is just a return to that. That is how evangelicals in the last century went astray in the 1840s and subsequently. That is precisely how it came about. Their argument was that they were merely out to defend the truth of the gospel against this increasing attack from the realm of natural science. And that was the method they adopted. They held that the Bible is only concerned with 'religious' truth and so, whatever science may discover, it cannot affect this truth.

Our friends today with the same motive – and let us grant that their motive is good and true – are doing exactly the same thing. It seems to me that in so doing they are on the same path as the followers of Ritschl and others, and it always ends in the same result, namely that the gospel itself is compromised. We must assert that we believe in the historicity of the early chapters of Genesis and all other biblical history.

Creation, Not Evolution

We accept the biblical teaching with regard to creation and do not base our position upon theories of evolution, whichever particular theory people may choose to advocate. We must assert that we believe in the being of one first man called Adam, and in one first woman called Eve. We reject any notion of a pre-Adamic man because it is contrary to the teaching of the Scripture.

Now someone may ask, Why do you care about this? Is this essential to your doctrine of salvation? Are you not falling into the very error of over-particularization against which you warned us at the beginning? I suggest that I am not, and for these reasons. If we say that we believe the Bible to be the word of God, we must say that about the whole of the Bible, and when the Bible presents itself to us as history, we must accept it as history. I would contend that the early chapters of Genesis, the first three chapters of Genesis, are given to us as history. We know that there are pictures and symbols in the Bible, and when the Bible uses symbol and parable it indicates that it is doing so, but when it presents something to us in the form of history, it requires us to accept it as history.

We must therefore hold to the vital principle, to which I have referred earlier, of the wholeness and the close inter-relationship of every part of the biblical message. The Bible does not merely make statements about salvation. It is a complete whole: it tells you about the origin of the world and of man; it tells you what has happened to him, how he fell and the need of salvation arose, and then it tells you how God provided this salvation and how he began to reveal it in parts and portions. Nothing is so amazing about the Bible as its wholeness, the perfect interrelationship of all the parts.

Therefore these early chapters of Genesis with their history play a vital part in the whole doctrine of salvation. Take for instance the argument of the apostle Paul in the Epistle to the Romans 5:12-21. Paul's whole case is based upon that one man Adam and his one sin, and the contrast with the other one man, the Lord Jesus Christ, and His one great act. You have exactly the same thing in 1 Corinthians 15; the apostle's whole argument rests upon the historicity. Indeed, it seems to me that one of the things we have got to assert, these days in particular – and it should always have been asserted – is that our gospel, our faith, is not a teaching; it is not a philosophy; it is primarily a history.

The apostles, you remember, on the day of Pentecost, filled with the Holy Spirit, were talking about the wonderful works of God. The works of salvation are God's acts! The Bible is a record of God's activity. Salvation is not an idea; it is something that results from actions which have taken place on the concrete plane of history. Historicity is a very vital matter. As I say, it is the very key to understanding the apostle Paul's elaboration of his doctrine of salvation.

In addition to that, of course, the whole question of the person of our Lord arises. He clearly accepted this history, he referred to Adam, and in speaking about marriage he clearly accepts the historicity of that portion of Scripture (Matt. 19:4-5). But quite apart from this, if you do not accept this history, and prefer to believe that man's body developed as the result of an evolutionary process, and that God then took one of these humanoid persons, or whatever you may call them, and did something to him and turned him into a man, you are still left with the question of how to explain Eve, for the Bible is very particular as to the origin of Eve. All who accept in any form the theory of evolution in the development of man completely fail to account for the being, origin, and existence of Eve. So there are scientific difficulties as well as these much more serious theological difficulties, but there is a general aspect to this particular matter which seems to me to be, in a sense, even more important.

These good friends who are thus, as they feel, safeguarding the Christian message of salvation by drawing this distinction are, I believe, doing precisely what the Roman Catholic Church did in connection with Copernicus and others. You remember how the Roman Catholic Church opposed the findings of these men. Why did she do so? Well, she did so because she was tied by Greek philosophical teaching with regard to the natural world. That teaching had come out of pure reason, not as the result of observation or of any scientific investigation. The philosophers had thought it through and they had laid down certain absolute propositions about the world and about the cosmos, so that when these scientific men came along and said that they had discovered this and that, it was rejected. Why? Because the church was not so much tied to the teaching of the Scripture as to the teaching of Aristotle and other Greek philosophers, and so she found herself in difficulties; she found herself denying what is truth and fact.

Now here, it seems to me, is the very thing that certain evangelical people are tending to do at the present time. They are tying themselves to modern, scientific teaching, and nothing is more dangerous than that. We must base ourselves exclusively on the Scriptures, and if this has always been true, it seems to me it is especially true today. We are living in an age of great change, great scientific change. The quantum theory and the work of Einstein have introduced a revolution into the whole realm of science. Take, for instance, the dogmatism with which the scientists spoke in the last century, how they talked about 'the absolute laws of nature', and so on, but they no longer do that, and they cannot do that. Everything today is indeterminate. Scientists now say that what we call the laws of nature are simply a very small section of the totality of truth. This is all we have discovered so far, but increasingly they are finding that their knowledge is very limited.

Modern science itself teaches us that we are not anti-scientific and we are not obscurantist if we do not accept statements as absolute truth and fact simply because they are made by certain prominent and great scientists. We know that great scientists have made very dogmatic statements in the past, which by now have proved to be wrong. They were teaching with great confidence, one hundred years ago, that the thyroid and the pituitary glands were vestigial organs, and people believed them. It was because they accepted such assertions that the faith of many evangelicals was shaken in the middle of the last century. Today we know that these assertions were wrong. All I am saying is that it is very dangerous for us to base our position, our exposition of the Scripture, upon the pronouncements of science. These are changeable, constantly moving. Indeterminacy is the rule today rather than determinacy, so we must be humble. And while we admit that we cannot explain everything and that there are certain things put before us for which we cannot account, what we must say is this: Because the Spirit has borne witness within us to the truth of the Scripture, we do believe that whatever is asserted in the Scripture about creation, about the whole cosmos, is true because God has said it, and though Scripture may appear to conflict with certain discoveries of science at the present time, we exhort people to be patient, assuring them that ultimately the scientists will discover that they have been in error at some point or other, and will eventually come to see that the statements of Scripture are true. Thus we base our position upon Scripture alone and this has always been the Protestant view of Scripture. There are two testimonies to the truth of the Scripture in all its parts: there is the external testimony of the Spirit in the word itself; there is the *testimonium Spiritus internum*, the internal testimony of the Spirit in us, giving us assurance that this is the word of God.[2]

You see the importance of the need to elaborate our doctrinal statements at the present time. There are some who

[2] Further on this subject, see D. M. Lloyd-Jones, *Authority* (1958; repr. Edinburgh: Banner of Truth Trust, 2015).

say, Yes, I accept it, I haven't changed my view at all on your basis of faith and what it says about the Scriptures. But when you talk to them in detail, you find that they have departed in this very serious, and I suggest, radical manner from the true position of the evangelical.

The Fall and Evil

We go on to assert that we must underline the fact of the historical fall of the first man, and that it happened in the way described in the third chapter of Genesis. Whether we can understand it or not is not the question. That is what we are told, and the apostle Paul in 2 Corinthians 11:3 reminds the Corinthians that 'the serpent beguiled Eve'. You cannot play fast and loose with these facts without involving the inspiration of the apostles, and, ultimately, the person of our Lord. You will soon be saying that he was a child of His own age, that he was ignorant in certain respects, and that he had simply the scientific knowledge of His own times, and so on. You begin to query and to question His statements, and ultimately you will have no authority at all.

Not only must we accept the historicity of Genesis 3 and its account of the fall. If you do not accept that as history, you are going to exclude from your belief one of the most amazing and comforting facts in connection with our faith, the proto-evangel of Genesis 3:15, the glorious promise that the seed of the woman shall bruise the serpent's head, the first prophecy concerning the virgin birth of Christ and how he was going to bring us this great deliverance. There is the first glimpse of the work, of the blessed work of the cross, all concretely stated in the historical account.

In the same way, we must assert the fact of the flood. I am not here making a complete statement, of course. Time prohibits that, but I am simply picking out certain things that we have to emphasize in a particular way at this present time. General statements are no longer enough. We must insist upon knowing what people believe in detail. We must test their statement that they accept the supreme authority of the Scriptures, and their trustworthiness in all these matters of faith and conduct.

Having dealt with our position on Scripture, we move on to certain other doctrines. Here also I want to make an addition to the basis of faith. I trust this will not surprise any of you. I am suggesting that we must make an assertion that we believe in the existence of the devil and his spirits. It is amazing to me that we do not say this. There are so many people who really do not believe in the existence of the devil and they do not believe in evil spirits. There are people known to us who are entirely orthodox, but if you start talking to them about devil-possession and exorcism, they show quite plainly that they think you are talking nonsense. They do not believe in the existence of evil spirits, or they tend to say that that was only true in the time of our Lord, a position which I find amazing and inexplicable.

There is here a twofold argument. They say that the gifts of the Spirit were confined solely to the apostolic age, and that they ceased with that age; and then by implication they seem to say that the devil was kind and polite enough to stop his activities also with the apostolic age. And so there is this utter confusion. No. We must assert that it is a part of our whole position that we believe in the supernatural realm, and in a spiritual conflict. Referring to this conflict, the apostle Paul writes, 'We wrestle not against flesh and blood, but against principalities, against powers, against the rulers of the darkness of this world, against spiritual wickedness in high places' (Eph. 6:12). How often even in evangelical circles do we hear this asserted at the present time? Is there not a tendency on our part to become intellectualists and to regard these truths as almost abstract? We talk so little about 'leadings of the Spirit' as the fathers used to, or 'prohibitions of the Spirit', and the wonderful activities of the Spirit, and we seem to avoid all talk of the activities of evil spirits, yet we are living in a world in which demon-possession seems to be coming back very rapidly, and even devil-worship and certain other terrible characteristics of the godless life.

So at this point we must assert our faith. We shall be regarded as fools. Any man who believes in the devil today is regarded as almost unintelligent, yet if you believe the Bible you must believe in this tremendous person and his awful power. The Bible, in a sense, is a record of the conflict between the forces of God and the forces of the devil, and we are told that this is to go on until the final destruction of the devil and all his forces.

Then we must go on to assert that man is spiritually dead, and that he is totally incapable of any spiritual good, 'dead in trespasses and sins' – not merely slightly defective – and that it is not true to say that he has it in him, if he only applies himself, to believe in God and to arrive at God. We must assert, as the Scriptures do, that man is totally dead, that the advances of science make no difference whatsoever to the fact that all men are 'by nature the children of wrath, even as others' (Eph. 2:3), that 'all have sinned, and come short of the glory of God' (Rom. 3:23).

One Way of Salvation

When we come to the doctrine of the atonement, we must underline in a very special way the substitutionary aspect and element of the atonement, the penal, piacular aspect. These are things that I find are most indicative of a man's position. An evangelical may say, Well, of course, I'm not a great theologian; I simply accept, I simply repeat the Scriptures' statements. And he does not want to tie himself down to the fact that there is this penal element in the atonement. He may say, All I know is that Christ's work, his sacrifice, puts me right with God. I suggest this is not enough. He is really excluding the whole of the Old Testament teaching with regard to sacrifice if he speaks in that way, let alone the particular and explicit statements made in the teaching of the apostle Paul. So we have to underline and emphasize this substitutionary element.

We must also assert in a very special way justification by faith alone, faith only. We have got to assert that justification is not the result of regeneration, nor does it depend upon our regeneration. That is the Roman Catholic teaching, that we are justified because we have been regenerated as a result of our baptism. This error can come in, and is cording in today in very subtle forms, but we must assert that God 'justifieth the ungodly' (Rom. 4:5), that it is entirely a forensic action, a legal pronouncement by God, and that we play no part whatsoever in it. This is the traditional evangelical teaching which we must assert.

The Church: Contemporary Issues

When we come to the church we must again make certain specific statements. I personally would assert that no evangelical can possibly believe in a state or territorial church. We know that these institutions came into being solely as the result of certain events in history. There is no suspicion of a suggestion of it in the New Testament, and how could there be? What is there about being born in a certain country which makes anybody a Christian? Why should the church be merely the spiritual aspect of the life of the state? It is remote from the teaching of Scripture and we know that of all elements in the history of the church, perhaps nothing has been productive of greater confusion than this whole notion of the state or territorial church. We believe in the communion of saints, and a church consists of saints; it is a communion of saints.

And, of course, in our basis we must believe in purity of doctrine – and we must assert this – and of sacraments. Therefore we must believe in discipline. There is no purpose in having a basis or a confession of faith unless it is applied. So we must assert the element of discipline as being essential to the true life of the church. And what calls itself a church which does not believe in discipline, and does not use it and apply it, is therefore not a true church.

But there are certain negatives here which must come in, and we must not minimize the importance of negatives. We must reject completely every notion of apostolic succession. We must reject the distinction between clergy and laity because it is not found in the New Testament. We must also reject the notion that bishops are essential to the life of the church. Now you may ask, What has this got to do with evangelicalism? I reply that certain evangelicals have been committing themselves to statements such as this: that we believe that the authority of bishops is identical with the authority of apostles, being the personal authority of the Lord. Two evangelicals have subscribed to that statement within the last year or so. Another statement they have given is that the bishop gives expression to the headship of Christ over His church. Where is the biblical authority for this? The answer is that there is none. This is the so-called 'development of doctrine'. The church in her experience and wisdom, they teach us, has found a suspicion of a suggestion of this notion implicit in the New Testament, and she has drawn it out. I suggest that we as evangelicals must reject this completely.

Coming to the sacraments, we must reject every suggestion of sacerdotalism. We do not believe in priests or any priestly action. We do not believe that the sacraments act in and of themselves; the term is *ex opere operato*. We do not believe that. So we must reject statements to which the same two evangelical writers mentioned above have committed themselves, that there is an efficacy inherent in the sacramental act itself. As evangelicals we reject that. There is no efficacy inherent in the sacramental act itself. A sacrament is nothing unless there is in the recipient belief. There is no efficacy inherent in the act itself. We do not believe in the sheer unqualified efficacy of sacraments.

I would not be calling attention to these matters were it not that these are statements made by evangelicals. This is an illustration of the tragic shift that has been taking place in the last ten years, and this is again opening the door to sacramentalism, sacramentarianism, and sacerdotalism. So we must assert very strongly that we reject any suggestion of baptismal regeneration. It must be entirely excluded, not only in the Roman Catholic form, but in every form. We must likewise reject any notion of sacrifice in connection with the Lord's Supper. There is no repetition of sacrifice there, no element of sacrifice. We must assert that all we offer in that sacramental act is ourselves. We reject that we offer anything at that point, save ourselves.

There, as I see things, are the additions and the elaborations which we must make today in view of the situation in which we find ourselves. This present basis of faith, as it is, is not enough; neither is any other. We have got to ask these specific questions. We have got to make sure that we are clear about these particular matters.

Secondary Truths Not Essential to Unity

That brings me to my next heading. I have been dealing so far with the essentials. I am still left with what I have called the non-essentials.

What do we mean by non-essentials? We are clear about these matters with which we have been dealing. We have been defining our evangelical position. But I have left unmentioned many other things outside our basis. What about them? I put them in the category of non-essentials. When I say that they are not essential, I do not say that they are not important. They are very important, and they must be discussed by evangelical people, but we must discuss them as brethren. As Calvin said, on such matters we ought not to divide but to try to help one another. We recognize our limits, our defects, our ignorance. We believe that promise of Paul's in Philippians 3 that even in these other matters, light will be given to us if we are patient and if we seek it together.

But we call them non-essential because they are not essential to salvation. This seems to be the test. Another reason I give for calling them non-essential is that they cannot be proved one way or the other. I do not say the Scriptures are equivocal, but there are matters upon which the Scriptures are not so clear that you can say this *must* be believed.

Then there is another reason for calling some of these things non-essential. Sometimes it is a question of understanding or lack of understanding, and we must always remember that we are not saved by our understanding. This is a most important point. Our danger as evangelicals is to fall into the trap of thinking that we are saved by our understanding; but we are not. Thank God, we are saved in spite of ourselves, in spite of our ignorance and everything else that is true of us. And sometimes the difference between evangelical people is entirely due to a difference of understanding. I will give you an illustration of it in a moment.

There is also a difference between a defective understanding and a positive denial of truth by able people. What I mean is this. You may have certain simple Christian people, not over-gifted with intelligence, who find it very difficult to understand some matters, but there are other men, able men, gifted men, highly intelligent men, who deliberately reject the same truths which the first group finds difficult to accept and understand. Those two positions are very different. While we are patient, sympathetic, and lenient with the first, we must condemn and separate ourselves from the second.

These are some of the reasons for drawing a distinction between essentials and non-essentials. Let me mention a few things, therefore, which I put into the category of non-essentials.

One is the belief in election and predestination. Now I am a Calvinist; I believe in election and predestination; but

I would not dream of putting it under the heading of essential. I put it under the heading of non-essential. Mark you, I would condemn Pelagianism; I would say that Pelagianism is a denial of the truth of the Scripture with regard to salvation – that goes out. But I am thinking of Arminianism in its various forms, and therefore I do not put this into the category of essential. I do not for the reason that this, for me, is a matter of understanding. You are not saved by your precise understanding of how this great salvation comes to you. What you must be clear about is that you are lost and damned, hopeless and helpless, and that nothing can save you but the grace of God in Jesus Christ and only him crucified, bearing the punishment of your sins, dying, rising again, ascending, sending the Spirit, regeneration. Those are the essentials.

Now when you come to ask me, How exactly do I come to a belief in this? I say that that is a matter of the understanding of the *mechanism* of salvation, not of the way of salvation. And here, while I myself hold very definite and strong views on the subject, I will not separate from a man who cannot accept and believe the doctrines of election and predestination, and is Arminian, as long as he tells me that we are all saved by grace, and as long as the Calvinist agrees, as he must, that God calls all men everywhere to repentance. As long as both are prepared to agree about these things I say we must not break fellowship. So I put election into the category of non-essentials.

Another matter I would put into the same category is the age and the mode of baptism: the age of the candidate, and the mode of administering the rite of baptism. I would put that again in the non-essential category for the same reason, that you cannot prove one or the other from the Scriptures. I have been reading books on this subject for the last forty-four years and more, and I know less about it now than I did at the beginning. Therefore, while I assert, and we must all assert, that we believe in baptism, for that is plainly commanded, yet we must not divide and separate over the age of the candidate or over the mode of administration. In the same way, we must not divide on the question of assurance of salvation.

We must not divide even on the question of church polity. I find it very difficult to say that, and yet I must say it. I am so opposed to this tendency today to insist upon bishops. This is what is being done by the ecumenical movement. You will find everywhere and in every country that bishops are made essential to the new church. You have it in South India, you have it in North India. This I resent and reject; but for the sake of evangelical unity among evangelicals, I would even be prepared to consider at any rate the possibility of some form of modified episcopacy for the sake of unity. I put it into the category of non-essentials for that reason.

In the same way, clearly, we must not divide on the question of prophetic interpretation: pre-, post-, a-millennialist, and so on. Not one of them can be proved, so we must not put them into the category of essentials. You have your views; hold them. Let us discuss them together; let us reason together out of the Scriptures; but if we divide on these matters, I maintain that we are guilty of schism. We are putting into the category of essentials what is non-essential. Evangelicals have sometimes done this. I remember a man telling me that he was 'doubtful' about the late Dr Gresham Machen, and he was doubtful of him for this reason: this man was very prominent in the World Fundamentalist Association, in which you had to believe in pre-millennialism, and because Dr Gresham Machen did not believe in pre-millennialism this man was doubtful about his evangelical position.

In the same way, there are beliefs with respect to the way of sanctification which are non-essential. There are rival theories held by equally good evangelicals which we put into the category of non-essentials. We hold our own personal views and hold them strongly; we believe that certain teachings are wrong; but it is not essential to salvation to believe the contrary. We are saved, and these good friends and ourselves will arrive in heaven in spite of our views on the particular mode of sanctification.

I would put into the same category the whole question of the baptism of the Spirit and the *charismata*, the spiritual gifts. There are differences of opinion here. I regard these as very important, but I would not venture to put them into the category of the essential.

There, as I see things at any rate, are some of these matters which we have to underline and emphasize at the present time. We have got to be clear and specific in establishing the evangelical position, but having done that, we must be very careful to draw this distinction between essentials and non-essentials lest we become guilty of schism and begin to rend the body of Christ.

May I close on this note. Our object in all this, as I say, is to safeguard the gospel, to keep the evangel clear, to be concerned about the salvation of men and women and the spread of the Christian church. Let that be our only motive. Let us have a single eye to the glory of God and of the Lord Jesus Christ. Let us realize always that we are all of us saved in spite of ourselves, that none of us is perfect in understanding or in any other respect, that not to be in fellowship with those who are born again is to be guilty of schism, which is sinful, that we are therefore called upon, as the apostle exhorted the Philippians, to stand in rank together, whatever the cost, whatever suffering may be involved, but always with this one idea that God may be over all, that God may be glorified, and that the name of Jesus Christ our Lord may be magnified among the peoples of the earth. Let us pray:

O Lord our God, we come to thee again, and we see what children we are, beginners battling on the edge of this great ocean of truth. Lord, give us, and keep us to, that simplicity that is in Christ. Keep us from being puffed up with knowledge and self-conceit and understanding. O God, give us ever a childlike spirit.

Deliver us from all false entanglements and intendments, and from every consideration save that thy name be magnified and made glorious, and that through even our feeble instrumentality many may be convicted of sin, converted, led to Jesus' blood and become members together with us of the body of Christ. So hear us, we pray thee, give us wisdom and circumspection in these evil days. Guide and direct those here present who are leaders of this work in various countries – Lord, we know that our sufficiency is of thee – and grant them to know that though they may at times feel lonely and isolated, with no one to help them and to stand with them, may they ever know that thou wilt never leave them nor forsake them. Grant that our confidence may ever be in thee and in the power of thy might. Bless thy servants as they commune together and meditate in the Executive and plan the future work. And in all the other meetings and activities of this day, we pray that all may experience thy benediction and thy grace. Pardon us, O Lord, for all the imperfection of our service and our every sin, as we ask these mercies, pleading nothing but the name and the merit of thy dear Son, our Lord and Saviour Jesus Christ. Amen.

ALSO
AVAILABLE FROM THE
BANNER OF TRUTH TRUST

Knowing the Times

ADDRESSES DELIVERED ON VARIOUS OCCASIONS 1942–1977

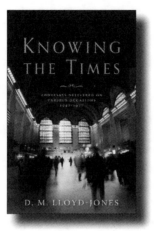

Martyn Lloyd-Jones' biblically informed insight gave a certain prophetic quality to his ministry; not in the sense that he foretold the future, but rather in his God-given ability to put his finger on the essential issues, and to apply the burden of God's word. *Knowing the Times* brings together a number of addresses which exhibit this vibrant prophetic character. Those who heard Dr Lloyd-Jones speak in a variety of contexts will easily recall the kind of impact which accompanied addresses like these. All will agree that *Knowing the Times* is one of the most significant Lloyd-Jones titles ever published. The addresses reprinted here remain 'tracts for the times'. The publishers believe that they have the potential to be used in the preparation of another generation who will be like the children of Issachar referred to in 1 Chronicles 12:32: 'Men that had understanding of the times, to know what Israel ought to do.'

ISBN 978 1 84871 277 5 | 400pp. | clothbound

The Banner of Truth Trust originated in 1957 in London. The founders believed that much of the best literature of historic Christianity had been allowed to fall into oblivion and that, under God, its recovery could well lead not only to a strengthening of the church, but to true revival.

Interdenominational in vision, this publishing work is now international, and our lists include a number of contemporary authors along with classics from the past. The translation of these books into many languages is encouraged.

A monthly magazine, *The Banner of Truth*, is also published. More information about this and all our publications can be found on our website or supplied by either of the offices below.

THE BANNER OF TRUTH TRUST

3 Murrayfield Road
Edinburgh, EH12 6EL
UK

PO Box 621, Carlisle,
Pennsylvania 17013,
USA

www.banneroftruth.org